DOLPHINS AND OUTLAWS

BRIAN MERRIKIN HILL

UNIVERSITY OF SALZBURG
1993

First published in 1993 by *Salzburg University* in its series:
Salzburg Studies in English Literature
Poetic Drama and Poetic Theory

89

Editors: JAMES HOGG and HOLGER KLEIN

Academic advisors: LEO TRUCHLAR and FRANZ ZAIC
Assistant to the editors: SABINE FOISNER

The editor is grateful to André Deutsch, London, for graciously permitting extracts from Humphrey Jenning's *Pandaemonium;* and to Carl Hanser Verlag, Munich, for an extract from Elias Canetti's *Human Province.*

ISBN: 3 7052 0802 0

Institut für Anglistik und Amerikanistik
Universität Salzburg
A-5020 Salzburg Austria

Distributed in the UK by: PENNINE PLATFORM, Ingmanthorpe Hall Farm Cottage, Wetherby, West Yorkshire, LS22 5EQ.

Distributed in the U.S.A. and Canada by Edwin Mellen Press, 240 Portage Road, Lewiston, New York 14092, U.S.A.

CONTENTS

Previous publications:
Wakeful In The Sleep Of Time (Taxus, 1984)
Local History (Littlewood, 1986)
The European Letters (Taxus, 1987)
(Still available from the author)

Eighteen Poems (Abbotsholme Press, 1947) and *Two Poems Of Pilgrimage* (Ruined Cottage Publications, 1977) are no longer available.

Acknowledgements:
Some of these poems first appeared in the following magazines and I am grateful to the appropriate editors: *The Adelphi, The New English Weekly, Outposts, The London Magazine, The Poetry Review, Prospice, Pennine Platform, The Poet's Voice, The Green Book, Orbis, Iron, Staple, Acumen, Nine, The Literary Review.*
Other poems have been printed in the following anthologies:
Poems of the Mid-Century (ed. John Holloway, Harrap)
Contemporary Yorkshire Poetry (ed. Vernon Scannell, Yorkshire Arts Association, 1984)

'Incantation at Ilkley' was commissioned for a Bronze Age Exhibition at Ilkley and Bradford.

'Le Dévot Christ' won the Yorkshire Open Poetry Competition 1977. 'The Make-Up Box' won the Scottish International Poetry Competition and the Hugh MacDiarmid Trophy in 1988, and 'The Human Variations' won the Scottish International Poetry Competition and the Hugh MacDiarmid Trophy, 1990. 'Indweller' was awarded a diploma in this competition in 1991 and printed in the anthology of commended poems. 'Slum Documentary — Shot 45' was printed in an anthology of poems commended in a York Open Poetry Competition.

Three of the 'Conversational Elegies for a Tyneside Kid' have been serialised in *Spectrum* and others are to follow.
'Bridge Over the Ouseburn' is to appear in *A Chaplet for Jesmond Dene* (Genera).

I would like to thank the Yorkshire Arts Association for two bursaries which eased some anxieties during the composition of some of these poems.

FOREWORD

WORDS ON THE WAY

I have been asked to give my own account of aims, influences and development and am glad of this because it enables some gratitude to be expressed where it is due. A critic in another magazine, considering my work as editor of *Pennine Platform,* said that my choice and outlook were of the Thirties; and this may be so, not because I am uncontemporary but because it was in the Thirties that I grew up. It is necessary that some beliefs, some values and some diagnoses, remain through all ages and do not change in accordance with journalistic or political fashion; an education minister recently criticised an opponent for using arguments of the nineteen-sixties, as though this dismissed them—apparently their validity as arguments was irrelevant! By now I am no longer interested in periodness or being pre-modern, modern, postmodern or post-modern, or even neomodern, but only in the validity of Poetry, a validity that can be found in Traherne, Pope, Arnold, Owen or Walcott and is something inherent and recognisable, nothing to do with contemporaneity or historical context.

At the age of eight, directed by a teacher called Miss Stockdale, I wrote a poem about Venice (which I knew only from photographs and descriptions), and from then on it somehow seemed that my destiny and calling was that of poet, though why this should be so and what it entailed were questions no one could have answered. I went on composing short lyrics on the ambiance of the Lincolnshire Marsh, on vague religious sentiments and somewhat imaginary loves.

What poetry could mean and be was established in my mind, I think, by the influence of Heaton Secondary School in Newcastle upon Tyne and the two teachers praised in the second 'Conversational Elegy', Ernest Dyer and Israel Simpson. A love of Shelley was then established, along with a powerful influence from French poetry, notably Lamartine, Hugo and Vigny, and a devotion to sculpted form created by Gautier, Leconte de Lisle and the Parnassians. When, many years later, while editing a New Soundings Radio programme, John Lehmann asked me for a poetic credo,

I said, to put Romantic emotion into Parnassian form. I thought
ud and high-falutin' but he found it convincing.

That interest in and passion for form have remained. Sound-echoes
such as *enact/reflect* give me an almost physical pleasure, and 'Shieldfield' in this book is one of the many poems that use the anarhyme invented
by the surrealist Steven Zivadin. The loose line of the 'Conversational
Elegies' and other poems is intended to be a form—and in the composition
the ear censored and commanded. It hovers between pentameter and
alexandrine and the beat, as in most English poetry, hovers between iamb
and anapaest. It suggested itself as the most suitable medium for writing
of that kind, since the first twenty or so lines appeared in the mind as they
now stand and established the rhythm of the work. Something in my
unconscious works at form, as is seen in 'Two Dreamt Sequences'

Modern criticism and theory have given undue importance to
language in the sense of contemporaneity of phrase, to the neglect of other
constituents of poetry—rhythm and emotive fluency— and also the union
of these elements with sound to create that undefinable music that is
characteristic of much verse that commands the allegiance of many
readers. Failure to recognise this music caused the peculiar contemporary
refusal to understand the popularity of A. E. Housman or some critics'
devotion to Edith Sitwell. The subtlety of rhythm is also strangely alien
to modern minds and ears. Some news readers, many politicians and even
the occasional actor fail to read a passage of prose with any attention to
its rhythm, even stressing words inaccurately—as, indeed, American
influences like the desire to rhyme adverbs with *merrily*, encourage. It is
said that even Dylan Thomas could not read Milton aloud with any
attention to prosody, and this failure of the ear is far too common. I
remember also hearing a poet asked about rhythm reply that he used
syllabics and did not concern himself with it; apparently French poetry,
which is syllabic, had no rhythm! I learnt better in my teens, reading Hugo
and Baudelaire.

Schooldays in Newcastle on Tyne made something that lasted long.
The love of Shelley, together with a passion for Blake—the whole
moderated by a fondness for Peacock— was nurtured by English teaching
of a high order by Miss Druller at Stourbridge Grammar School, and it

was a person so formed that went to Oxford in 1935.

A life, however, is not linear in one stream but beginning in various tributaries flows in channels and distributaries like the Withern Eau as it approaches the sea at Saltfleet Haven. One tributary is related in the 'Conversational Elegies' and the poems 'A Dangerous Sympathy' and 'Shieldfield'; one distributary is the thinking that led me to preach in various Methodist chapels and think of becoming an Anglican priest; it is not surprising that the two came together much later in the poems to the Blessed Virgin and St. Mary Magdalene in *Wakeful In The Sleep Of Time*; the coming together seems to have been established at Héas, where a visit had a remarkable effect, though I did not know at that time that Notre Dame de Héas was a Black Virgin and would not then have attached much importance to the fact. The Muse (one shape of many names) existed in various bodies and various guises, as in 'Litany In November':

> Lady who may not exist but if you do not
> Whose live benevolence must be assumed so that
> There seems to be hope of light—
>
> Lady whose understanding is tenderly amoral
> Virgin, Magdalen, Isis and Dancing Girl
> Whose mysteries
> Are inscrutable, beyond
> Physics, Biology, metaphysics
> And every irrefutable argument of the professional wise—
>
> Lady of the rocks
> And of the clay, of
> Flesh, mud, or iridescent
> Crystal of the broken vase
> And clear luminous
> Grail on the altar imagined
> Beyond this marsh that reeks barren because polluted
> Bordered by sludged gravel
> Where the tern dies with the fish
> And the sea
> Sluggishly, threateningly moves
> Blunt waves to prolong extinction—
> Now we are lost, sitting

In the mind's middle range, concerned
With what seems real—the international
Beauty contest or the skinless sores
Of refugees who, also beautiful,
Wait impolitic on the sea of nowhere—
Flesh exultant or suffering
Photographically distanced, casually
Noticed as time passes
To palimpsest our private grief
Which if revealed, X-rayed,
Would not obscure
Mankind and men unkind and children dying—

My mind was formed by a Christian Socialist upbringing and a
devotion to Shelley, whose work in verse and prose I had read by my
sixteenth birthday. This mind grew up in circumstances described in the
Note at the end of *Wakeful In The Sleep Of Time:*

Part of my childhood was spent in Newcastle upon Tyne when ninety
per cent of the population of Jarrow was unemployed. My father, a
Methodist minister and early Christian Socialist, working for the
Labour Party when it first gained the parliamentary seats of Seaham
Harbour, Don Valley and Belper, suffered the disapproval of the richer
laymen for his efforts towards social justice; he ran an illegal newspa-
per during the General Strike of 1926 and I still remember the sound
of the duplicators working through the night. I also remember the
poverty of Shieldfield (where my little girl-friend could not come out
to see me if her only dress was being washed and where Methodist
dignitaries failed to observe that many children had no shoes); the
procession of the sick at Belper begging my father for a 'recommend'
to get into hospital; the poverty and the epidemics of smallpox and
diphtheria at Worksop.

The influences on my social and political thinking became those of
Shelley, Kropotkin, Péguy, Herbert Read, Ivan Illich, Heinrich Böll
and Halldór Laxness (whose late novel *The Atom Station* moves me to
tears if I just think of it). Only for about three weeks did I succeed in
being a Marxist. Most of my life I have been a pacifist and an anarchist,
conscious that governments are not now and never have been the
creation of the people but the descendents of the imposed power of the
violent and rich. I am not a practical anarchist because anarchism is
impractical, but I think that every effort should be made to use govern-

ments for the benefit of the poor, the oppressed and the deprived: governments have no other legitimate functions anyway. Experience in the care and rescue of delinquent and maladjusted children has convinced me that few of them are to be blamed—few human beinhgs are ever to be blamed, only those who wield power willingly or exalt fictions like the nation-state, the working classes, professionalism, 'the town', 'the country' etc. over the individual—who should be left to live, love, suffer and rejoice in peace. Most organisations seem to prevent human beings from living on the earth, with it and recognising it as their home. The earth is man's hard home; the 'world' as made by man in his folly is becoming his prison.

The thoughts in the second of those paragraphs obviously result partly from four years at Oxford (which I loved and where I benefited from the influence of F. C. Horwood, C. S. Lewis, various devout Quakers, a Methodist study group and sundry Welsh Nationalists) and long years spent in teaching. I became a teacher to earn money so that I could be a poet, and almost forgot the aim in the activity. But that career, having created the outlook in 'The Bridge', ended with the disaster that generated 'Marram', though I did spend some five years in state schools after leaving the independent sector I mainly served in, and this fed my concern to deliver vulnerable and lovable children from a soul-destroying materialism compared with which Marxism is over-spiritual. The present crime-rate would seem to indicate that something is sadly wrong with the nature of our upbringing of children, but the fault lies in the 'ethos' of the society they grow up in; my experience of state education led me to respect the dedication of those teachers who were my colleagues.

The educational tradition in which I worked (I began at Abbotsholme, the *fons et origo* of the 'progressive' and spent many years at Wennington) was, I suppose, semi-Pelagian and optimistic in outlook, but no one who has worked with children in this century can neglect the concept of original sin and Newman's theory of the 'aboriginal calamity' that has riddled the universe with evil, Boehme's idea of a resistance in the material with which the human spirit works and Koestler's finding that human nature has a flaw that prevents its expected progress. It is surprising that critics should find Shelley lacking in recognition of evil; they ignore 'The Cenci', 'The Sensitive Plant', the analysis of human corruption in 'The Triumph Of Life' (which in one text talks of 'the mutiny within'), the self-criticism of 'Adonais' and the self-disgust in some of the poems of depression. These critics are often people who think they accept a Christian view of 'fallen man'—but in their understanding of Christianity they strangely ignore that Christ came to save and that Christianity promises redemption. Thus they do not understand 'Prometheus Unbound' as a myth of redemption; the fallen state of the universe is decribed in harrowing detail and its state in redemption is in strong contrast to what the poem saw as characterising the real world, in which many people

> Dare not devise good for man's estate,
> And yet they know not that they do not dare.
> The good want power, but to weep barren tears.
> The powerful goodness want: worse need for them.
> The wise want love; and those who love want wisdom;
> And all best things are thus confused to ill.
> Many are strong and rich, and would be just,
> But live among their suffering fellow-men
> As if none felt: they know not what they do.
>   'Prometheus Unbound' I.1, (623-31)

These words are strangely prophetic of Yeats's

> The best lack all conviction, while the worst,
> Are full of passionate intensity
>   'The Second Coming'

I think that Yeats must have been thinking and possibly improving on Shelley's lines.

My mind found no contradiction between a Christian view and the plot and fourth act of 'Prometheus Unbound'; indeed a combination of Blakean vision and Jungian understanding supported a hopeful interpretation of the human individual and human society. This harmonious view was, however, to be shattered by the economic evil of Western Society—the right-wing backlash destructive of rational values and genuine humanitarian caring. And, as Shelley realised, a corrupt society corrupts the minds and attitudes of those who grow up in it, so that rebellion against evil can become also evil or defective and a prey to what it opposes.

The real thinking of Shelley has been seriously underestimated, even in his bicentennial year. On an earlier anniversary Doris Lessing complained about identical tepid articles by dons from various universities, and 1992 seems to have replaced these by simple neglect. But had 'Laon and Cythna' (or 'The Revolt Of Islam') been shorter and not had a woman revolutionary leader and a brother-and-sister incest element, it could have been a formative prophetic document, even forecasting the fascist backlash, and been valued even by the T. U. C. Establishments and other arguments that claim Shelley as a Platonist rather than a politician neglect a point made by Fred Beake that it was because he was a Platonist that he was a revolutionary: and writing him off as an 'airy-fairy' (Oxley's phrase) Platonist, battered angel, etc. has failed to obscure the genuine thoughtful conviction, though

> Away, away from men and towns
> To the wild woods and the downs

figured more largely than 'The Mask Of Anarchy' and the epilogue to 'Prometheus Unbound'. Recently, of course, there has been a new treason of the clerks, in which intellectuals, confessedly or otherwise, have deserted the true British radical tradition and consented to inhabit a Thatcherite or Post-Thatcherite atmosphere and have taken refuge in a negative escapism of the kind found in the later work of Philip Larkin. The contrast to this capitalist materialism has often been a narrow Marxism which may find it difficult to see Blake and Shelley in true focus. The reaction against Marxism and radical thought has often been to lump all 'left-wing' thinkers with detestable Stalinist tyranny or write them off as wishy-washy libertarians. It is significant that a recent interest in political poetry centred on anti-communist poems of Eastern European origin and imitations of them, and ignored the English and French tradition and the works of Neruda, Carpentier, Vallejo and others in Central and South America and the achievement of Aimé Césaire. Articles by distinguished and presumably knowledgeable critics assumed that students and even fellow-scholars would acquiesce in the assumption that Blake and Shelley had never written a line. How many of them would have recognised the literary allusion of Owen's 'Strange Meeting' if older persons had not told them? And could they read Owen, anyway? One is driven to the conclusion that respected critical writers and English dons omitted to read a considerable part of the syllabus; this is possibly why they spend so much time writing in the Sunday papers to bourgeoisify attitudes or discussing literary theory in language that reads like a parody of academic discourse and is as illuminating as the droning translation of the speech of a Soviet fraternal delegate. Paul Foot set about a vigorous redressing of the balance and showed to what depths of hypocrisy the rich establishment will go to defend itself against what it may feel to be betrayal by dissidents. Other contemporary critics, notably Richard Holmes in his biography, have gone far to correct the blurring of Shelley in an over-ethereal mist. What some Shelleyans set in contrast to Arnold's ineffectual angel was often a being of great passion for justice but little power of genuine thought. And there has been some confusion in the interpretation of nineteenth century language and thought-forms: the heavily criticised belief in the perfectibility of man may in fact have been merely a belief in human progress—though this belief, of course, neglected his own realisation of the coming backlash and his knowledge of the effects of the 'aboriginal calamity'. A new school of Shelley students, as perceptive and thorough as the Blake academics, is needed to achieve a balanced and authoritative interpretation. My own mind was too formed by Shelley to achieve the clear-sightedness such scholars could have, but the effect on my thinking and work is evident. Scholars could begin by establishing why Yeats's allegiance to Shelley was stronger than his attachment to Blake, and how thinking about poetry could have been different if Yeats had been followed rather than F. R. Leavis.

Those other influences mentioned in the note to *Wakeful In The Sleep Of Time* which I have quoted modified and supplemented the Christian and Shelleyan urge towards redemption, and the self-imposed translation of Saint-Pol-Roux and Pierre Emmanuel also deepened the thinking and the hopes. My search for Saint-Pol-Roux, provoked by the dedication of Vercors' *Le Silence De La Mer*, led me to a *poète-mage* of considerable depth and wisdom. In many ways a precursor of surrealism, though in others the victim of nineteenth-century optimism about progress, Saint-Pol-Roux intensified my concern for the suffering (the Kid from Savoy influenced the Tyneside Kid), together with my devotion to St. Mary Magdalene and my feeling, so apparently out of place in the present age, that God is not dead but in the process of being born. It was David Gascoyne who joined to this an appreciation of Pierre Emmanuel by sending me 'Magdalen In The Garden', which led to an obsessive translation of *Chansons du dé à coudre*, the only book of Pierre's that I could at first locate. It was he himself who introduced me to the great Biblical epic dramas and *Le livre de l'homme et de la femme*. In *Le grand oeuvre* I found a faith similar to that of Saint-Pol-Roux—a belief in the gradual unfolding of God in the development of the cosmology. Pierre Emmanuel had probably a greater sympathy with the oppressed and victims of evil in our age than anyone else, but still held his belief in the triumph of the good, the coming of redemption and the realisation of the divine in the human.

These ideas and hopes fortified me in my concern for education and my belief in the mission of the teacher. Our present age, of course, suffers from governments with little belief in education and little concern for the welfare of children and their unfettered development (as is to be expected of 'thinkers' who believe in human evil rather than redemption). But these obscurantist delusions must surely pass away.

My career in teaching may have hindered the writing of poetry (though I had been published by Philip Mairet in *The New English Weekly*, in *The Adelphi* under Ifor Evans, Howard Sergeant's *Outposts, The Poetry Review, The London Magazine* and Peter Russell's *Nine*, and in an anthology *Poems of the Mid-Century* edited by John Holloway) but it deepened knowledge and understanding. A teacher in another independent school, having heard me praised for leading the young to like Louis MacNeice, asked me where I began—with the ballads and poems of action, to work slowly forwards, or how? I replied that I began with Louis MacNeice and worked backwards to Owen, Yeats, Shelley, Blake, Pope and Shakespeare. In all this I was greatly influenced by Eliot as interpreter of his religious pilgrimage, MacNeice as vivid recorder of an age and defender of innocence, and Edwin Muir as one who saw the story of life as comprehensible only in terms of what he called the fable. For all these poetry was an art concerned with life, as for me it still is. Later I found in Hugh MacDiarmid another powerful mind who thought about politics and living in vast sweeps of analysis and comprehension. I also found more modern French poets such as Reverdy, whom I discovered when visiting the Ecole des Roches in Normandy and assisting in the recreation of an English section in its library almost immediately after the war. I was stirred by Reverdy's realisation of the evanescent, the inconsequent and the mysterious and by his desire that the world should be comprehensible as a universe with God in it to alleviate the evil and suffering, and his search for something in reality that would replace the nothingness created by the collapse of his religious faith and his resultant disbelief in God. Anna Balakian in *Surrealism: the Road to the Absolute*, noting the dullness of many of the landscapes among which Reverdy lived, described his work as 'the triumph of inscape over landscape'.

The generation of modern poets that might have been expected as influences—Hughes, Larkin, Heaney etc.—were in reality my contemporaries or came after me—after all, I was first published in 1942—and of American poets it was the established, like Whitman, or others like Vachel Lindsay and e.e.cummings who figured in my mind, not later and better known luminaries. I would, in fact, protest against the linear historicism of much contemporary criticism. Warped, it produces such absurdities as a school anthology which pointed out the non-Words-worthianism of Ted Hughes! Even sane, it moves from Auden, through attacks on Dylan Thomas, to the Movement and ignores David Jones and Basil Bunting. A Guardian critic once foolishly set Walcott in context as combining Yeats and Larkin (presumably a native could only imitate the metropolitan). The allegedly historical view also ignores the immense achievement of one of Britain's most important poets, Tony Harrison. Linear historicism cannot fully recognise the importance and significance of Geoffrey Hill, Vernon Watkins, R. S. Thomas, Charles Causley and James Fenton, all of whom at various times could have been regarded as leading poets, and who certainly had an influence on my thought and practice. In some ways I am more in the world of R. S. Thomas and Jack Clemo than in that of contemporary literary chatter.

Others who do not figure in literary histories, such as Andrew Young and Ruth Pitter, also deserve a tribute. And I remember that at the time of a contest for the leadership of the the Labour Party, Roy Hattersley delighted the chattering critics by expressing his admiration for Philip Larkin (in spite of political disagreement) and Neil Kinnock earned derision by favouring Idris Davies. I had treasured Idris Davies for many years and his *Gwalia Deserta* affected the 'Conversational Elegies', having, incidentally, passed into ephemeral folklore as the source of a 'folksong' by Pete Seeger about the sad bells of Rhymney. There is a humanity in Idris Davies lacking in the hyped performers this age praises. I would also like to praise and thank Adrian Mitchell, but he had no part in my poetic development and no one, least of all a retired English teacher, can imitate him. His humanity and universal sympathy make a strong appeal. The social passion that responds to Davies and Mitchell was, of course, partly shaped by Auden, especially by poems that he later omitted from the canon. Those of my age grew up in an atmosphere of Auden (before he became curmudgeonly and quirkily conservative) and I treasure works now forgotten, such as 'The Quest' published in 1941 together with 'New Year Letter'.

After I left teaching I was greatly supported by the Pennine Poets group, that contained widely different poets, each able to make a notable contribution—Cal Clothier, Mabel Ferrett, Stephen Henderson Smith and others provided not only encouragement but wise counsel, as did Anna Adams and John Ward; the first had a command of artistic craftsmanship and the second skilful language of social realism and intellectual honesty. These for me succeeded the group at Knottingley under the leadership of Christopher Pilling, whose concern for the professionalism of poetry served me well. Poetry is in fact a collection of rivers like those of the Yorkshire Dales, not one stream with successive landscape characteristics like the Tyne. One can admire and learn from Shelley, Blake, Auden, MacNeice, Kathleen Raine and Derek Walcott without classifying them or listing them in periods or football league tables. I once presented a sixth form with anonymous extracts from Arnold, Eliot, Auden, Larkin and Hughes and asked who stirred them most and who (in Quaker phrase) spoke to their condition—the unanimous answer was Matthew Arnold. The contemporary poets who appeal to me most are Milosz and Walcott, though I still remember the influence of Lascelles Abercrombie, Wilfred Gibson, David Jones, Basil Bunting and Herbert Read—some of whom may seem mere names now, even if that. It must be strange for people whose minds are full of Hughes, Heaney, Larkin and Simon Armitage to meet someone whose roots and thoughts remember Traherne and Reverdy. Two important inspirations I have insufficiently praised are David Gascoyne and Kathleen Raine. To the former I have paid tribute in numerous articles and his early poems, especially *Ecce Homo*, helped to set the tenor of my poetic ways. Kathleen Raine also encouraged by publishing translations of Pierre Emmanuel and approving some of my activities. I remember her replying to my hope to save the world through poetry that she hoped to save poetry from the world; but I persist in the thought given in *Wakeful In The Sleep Of Time*: 'Modern society seems to me mainly to be a machine for the elimination of mankind. I inherit the Methodist (and Shelleyan) urge for the salvation of man.' And I believe that poetry is part of the defence of the human spirit. The Scholar Gypsy expected a message from the divine that never seemed to come. I believe in the mission of poetry in a way that modern wits and entertainers may not understand. And I still echo Reverdy: 'One can believe in God without loving him ... but one can love him without believing in him—with a love insane, rebellious and strong, loving all that he might have been if he could have been'. And as a tribute to a great inspiration I have not listed I add from St. John Perse: 'And it is enough for the poet to be the guilty conscience of his time.' I am grateful that some of my contemporaries who have nobly shouldered this burden or who may have unintentionally served in this duty have been more successful than I have. I have but to repeat, from *Wakeful in the Sleep of Time:*

CONFITEOR

Pardon, voices and angels,
Deafened by wrangles when thought
Sickened dissolute and words
Went whoring to smooth lords
In lighted palaces, I stood mute
In gathering darkness by the gate.

Forgive, outcries and spirits.
Prisoned by merit in a room
Double-glazed by dream against the cold
That ambushed a child's limbs on the high wold,
In the warm vale I lit the gleam
That led but, curtained, left to doom.

Take me, daimons and angers,
Safe past dangers to the rock
Against waves' crack spined hard,
Far from neon and the bribed guard,
To grasp with drowning hands as tide pulls back
Dolphins and outlaws native to crest and wrack.

Brian Merrikin Hill
Ingmanthorpe Hall Farm Cottage
Wetherby
West Yorkshire
LS22 5EQ

for Irene

I

EARLIER POEMS

THE BRIDGE*

I

Like boats of tulip petals moments float
windhazarded by words on waves of time;
driven to imaginary quays remote
from life, they wither on a beach of slime
by the pond's edge in memory. The plant
lives by abandoning its beauty, but we
would unnaturally perpetuate each petal, grant
each moment a detached eternity—
lacking the faith to save through winter danger
our joy from time, the offended world's avenger.

II

Young I frightened of bridges
dizzying high over brown tide-swirling river
or single planks over ditches
between marsh fields where reeds mud-rooted quiver,
lived familar with houses,
island pasts moated from the highroad world
where future-stepping horses
clopped towards tower and steeple whose pulled bells pealed
their peace-full matins of promise. The dyke flowed, spanned
by parallel presents from garden to peopled land.

---

* The basic landscapes are those of the Lincolnshire Marsh near the villages of
Conisholme and Saltfleet, where from inland roads Spurn Head Lighthouse is clearly
visible at night; the city of Newcastle upon Tyne; Morfa Harlech; and the head of the
Nant Ffrancon (valley of the beaver) near Llyn Ogwen. Other landscapes occur: that of
Cornwall on the edge of Bodmin Moor near King Doniert's Stone in St. Cleer; Galloway
near Gatehouse of Fleet—though the single-span bridge is over the water of Minnoch near
Glen Trool; Morar, where out of a deep lake flows one of the fastest and shortest rivers
in the world; and the upper part of Great Langdale, where the interested may search for
the islanded holly tree. The rebuilt church of St. Melangell is at Pennant Melangell, near
Llangynog. The cold apple blossom weather was in Kent.

On a fenced bridge lonely and single
young I leaned to gaze on slow-moving water
waving the reed-green jungle
gently as roach swam hiding from waiting slaughter.
The road bridge easy and friendly,
populous, dropped to dark mud at open edges;
beneath it, unwatched, too blindly
the roach strayed where pike lurked under the arch's
oblique reflection in luminous black. Time grudges
the guarded present, favours precipitous ledges.

In cold apple-blossom weather
older in southern sheltering hills I pondered
thoughts of where bleak gulls gather;
reed-whistling marsh; sands where breakers thundered,
long linear furls of threat;
through the far miles' flat dark the lighthouse flashing;
tide rippling in creeks as the moon set;
lone dawn over hollowed dunes with marram rustling;
the sea beyond the ribbed beach in deep runs rushing,
O level world, to a child without limit—the bright
air glistened, the road was Eden, the fields green light.

III
I recall when walking
this dyke-edged road
once awaking
in a vision made
by mind or nature
where all became
past, present, future
a single flame.

Now reeds wilt yellow
as I stand by a cracked

4

unlovely sallow
and I suspect
light that pervaded
all things that were
not gone or faded
but never there.

What's true? I know
of a poem which made,
two deaths ago,
an arrowlike road
a bright line, stark
from hill to sea
but now grown dark
means nothing to me.

In a flash some day
two deaths ahead,
I may see with joy
what now blind I read,
an imprisoned fable
escape to end
with me able
to comprehend.

IV

High over Tyne, that brown tide-swirling river,
alone I stood midway from child to man
seeing only appealing water, never
replacing always, ignoring the steel span
the arch suspending a road on which men travelled
over the sea-going ships who made this death
by their buoyant adventure a path—
but the body cavilled

5

till the mind found better reason, in lung salt breath
cleared for the eyes wide vision and the soul marvelled.

Living I found streams stone-impeded hastening
in triumph of foam and coruscant smooth curve
bridged by stone-trestled slabs on moors whose swerve
of hill's cut by gaunt-standing mica-glistening
cross or king's stone; by single peaceful arch
where mountain waters pound rocks to be free
in the yellowgray Galloway sea;
or, where white birch
clings to bank stones with roots that clasp and search,
by stepping stones near the islanded holly tree.

Between bends the road crosses the turbulent falls
hustling blue Morar to the lucid strait.
The driver glimpses red weed, white beach, recalls
the guidebook: "More silver sand. Did you see the boat?
The lake is up that road to the right, dead end
far off the route. Can you hear the torrent roar?"
They pass on, they ignore
the source, life's ground—
that calm baptismal water lapping the strand,
the mysterious holy hills of the further shore.

V

I walked alone along a marshland road
when no voice spoke,
silence created meaning, nothing made
what words shall not revoke
nor all things unmake.

Real are recollections
but how real what is recollected?
Revisiting the small town loved in childhood

6

we are amazed to find narrow
the streets remembered broad.
It is as though a part of reality
had gone out like a candle
in the draught of time.

Should I desert the dream, content to have acted
honestly by the painful world, the shallow
realist abrogation of the gentle
as characterising a loved home
destroyed by enemy action?
The thought to which all others tend
but which we do not comprehend
sufficiently to justify
our resignation is that try
as best we can to snap the gleam
that interpenetrates the stream
of life, we make an album print
lightlessly false but so exact
that we deny the vital glint,
mistaking photograph for fact.
Movement creates the zest
we fail to analyse at rest.

VI
Quiet among the rounded hills
that face the east and feed with snow
the limpid pebble-happy rills
that merge to make the Tanat flow,

Melangell's shrine has been rebuilt:
new stones support the ancient there;
still from her kindness to the hare
springs love redeeming careless guilt.

A simple action resurrects
light which time dowsed. Men recreate
from bits grass-hid by brambled fate
life the importunate world rejects.

VII
Now I far from that orient level land
(having crossed peaks like raven's cries, that move
against the dizzying sky, look down
on vast lakes in broad vales yet seen as patches
of water in thin clefts) arrive
at this small hillside-clasping town,
Harlech, whose castle watches
across its different but familiar marshes
new wind-adzed gale-planed dunes of western sand.

The sun makes time by bridging space, the day
arches from sea to sea, each minute spans
a reedy dyke, a thundering cataract,
or river meandering on its gentle way,
each echoing other as each keystone scans
what long or briefly flashed the stream reflects,
mirror after mirror varying constant theme,
angles of thought in fact and truth in dream,
fabric of new and old each hour constructs.

We have not lost paradise; it was never found.
We are always seeking, looking into our dim
childhood memories, like a boy on the sand
who has lost a sixpence—important only for him,
since the waves creep nearer, the people pass, going home,
and his parents angrily call.
                                        We may once have been
unconsciously there by that eternal stream
when, ignorant of maps, with no camera, alone
and so very young, we visited a valley,

round-felled and sounding-watered, to play by a mill.
But the ordnance survey shows us our memory's folly:
the orientation is different, the wooded hill
that we loved from the speedwell banks of the pebbly leat
was really elsewhere, the mill ruined. Do you remember,
we spoke to the miller whilst we watched the sun set?
Apparently in the north.
                  We have reached this sombre
land from a sunlit country that did not exist,
and our eyes are familiar with light that did not shine
except in memory: a magical twist
of a glass has flooded the past with tomorrow's sun.

And always we live in today, but we can never
know what it is till as yesterday it resembles
the village we left behind us, to clamber over
this col to the future valley, where paradise trembles
like water seen distantly blue, muddy when reached.

We have not lost paradise; it was never found.
It cannot be left, or dwelt in, or approached.
It is life in the unextinguished light of mind.

    VIII
Craig braich tu du,
the black side of the crag's arm
which threatens the bridge
between the lake-filled farming valley
and the precipitous pass
sacred to the extinct beaver,
is a spur of the mountain
called Pen yr oleu wen—

Headland of the white light.

MARRAM[*]

In memoriam Tarjei Vesaas.

"Our God is that which is left
when all Gods have been listed
and marked No, not him, not him."
                                                Halldór Laxness.

In hollowed dune,
Grass, root and rise.
Keen-edged, find death-fraught wind,
Bend, curl and sing.

Create from salt
Eroding sea
Brief pregnable
Fertility.

Let these words murmur. Here is the place
Sea-made, sea-broken. To sandhills at haven's end
Where in wind's song, waves' beat
In a boy nothing became I, now I ageing
Empty come. Here I began
With symbol as idol—the 'eternal'

---

[*]   The landscape is that of Saltfleet Haven, which when I revisited it had been changed
by the breaking of a sea-bank. The Withern Eau, which rises in the Wolds, flows out to
sea there. The peacock seen on the way back from the dunes is a poetic licence—and this
licence continues. The Northern City is Newcastle upon Tyne. In the Welsh story of
Branwen the daughter of Llyr, seven men carried the head of the Blessed Bran towards
London, but they paused for eighty years at Gwales in Penfro (Pembrokeshire) charmed
by the singing of three birds into forgetting all their misery. They remembered their misery
and that of the world when Heilyn opened the third of three doors, that which looked
towards Cornwall. The birds of Rhiannon had this effect on people, and she was for a
time the wife of Pwyll, prince of Annwn, which is the underworld. The whole story is in
The Mabinogion.

10

Has now changed. But I'm still enthralled
By sandflat, saltmarsh, dune
Guarding vulnerable levels inland far
To border of blue wold. Thought strong like tumbling river
In those chalk hills now shifts like tiderun's course;
Ideas men bought make a cross on the map 'Chapel (site of)';
But personal acts, rooting like sea-lavender,
Quicken a heart the marketing world rejects.

By dead babies,
Lovers severed like limbs,
Comes peace triumphant
To statesmen.

Moon shining on rose quartz
Does not ask
The reflection to be paid for.

Daffodils by rusting scrap
Illuminate not wilt at
Where they are.
In that mean town, far off
Beside a murkier sea
Children may prove
Flowers brave as brief
And men, like twisted thorn
Which drops to area mud
Berries as red as death,
Jewel with iridescent act
Corroded streets that intersect
Like sword or cross.

Father, released at last
To care again for sons theft fed,
Search though in vain,

Warders devalue saints, but men
Know the divine has human hands.

Dark girl, speak urgent-eyed your
Dull trivia. Thoughtful
Are arms, thighs, hands.
Seeing a pretty friend desert
The date arranged,
You turned back—ready.

Beside the murderer's grave
Suave men told his mother
Of God's purpose.

Incandescence of compassion,
Be not photo flash
But perpetual light.

Do away with idols. Do not break them
With sacred hammers; take them
To a quiet tip by night. Return
To sleep in unconcern.

Pain ends unexpectedly but may resume
Or change, subsume
Itself into man's pathos. Isolate—
Madden. Accept a general fate,

Commune of suffering and dispossessed;
Forget in society. Let the heart harden
Only because of the insane distressed
Abolished by what none can pardon.

World divides. Wake with the lamb
While lion, butcher, priest

Prowl righteously.

Lest, forgetful by this quiet haven,
As those in Gwales lulled by divine music—
Who would have stayed, neglecting grief and innocence—
We do not open the Cornish door
To burdened travel.

Ages of strife ago
Nekura's tomb
Taxed in twelve towns
Grandsons of starveling men
Whipped dead to build it.

Their proud inheritors,
The men we know,
Live in tall blocks of cells
That point towards
Fouled stratosphere where new
Pharaoh and treasurer fly
To plan their poverty.

Famed undying birds
Charm to stark grave
Miner, like slave
Of megalith.
Rhiannon
Was queen to death: her priests
Chant Egypt's radio song
To faithful ears.

Featured as news for opulent rooms
From roadside mud
A legless child, dark-eyed,

13

Stretches to seek
Her father.

By hill track mythless
Battle cross—
What story lost
Like pain of women.

Legends that live, like ours,
Survive the cold
Of loss, dispel
The truth of pain,
Bereave the alone
Again.

For dead sons men build
No monuments that house
Eyes to guide feeling hands.
Tears of hot salt
Scalded the sentient cheek
Of hero's child, pallid
As snowdrops on dumb coffin.

Then, as now,
Present illuminates
Past, but trek
From light and
Shadows fall forward:

Now, as then.

Travelling by train
After long talk with those
Deemed maladjusted,
Whom an involved tautness made

Temperate, sincere,
I saw Grantham spire,
Elegant, upright,
Under whose queenly beauty
Measured conventional forgiveness
Lulls the self-satisfied.
But before that,
A windswept half-tree,
Branchless, its heart wood naked,
Shaped, torn, sculpt,
Shone like Christ
Inclining gold in the sun.

Wind stirring transient dune
Now before storm
What are your gifts?

Stamen, whorled leaf, berry,
Feather of gliding wing,
Shell pearled like flesh;
Seed of the knotted grass
Message of spreading root
That guards where now I go.

Peacock, in clear sunlight
Confront statesman-priest. In drizzle
Visit poets.

Creatures of elder seas
Death ignorant crushed
In stone delight us now:

Art can impersonate
Time, invent
Fossils mocking grief.

Yet through this weight of world,
For present pain,
Strongly be with mankind.

Not for flower-mart, altar
Or gallery vase
Did this fuchsia bloom
Red and purple in the soft wind
Waving message to bee and butterfly.

Girl in marsh garden,
Turn your fuchsia lips
To glint ensorcelling moon.

Go within quiet walls
Whence building martin sees
Two tamarisks thrive.

Leave open on the evening mantelpiece
Letters that morning
Recasts.

FOR A FAREWELL

This our history
bitter like metal
stirs with a beauty like
the rose's petal.

Nothing will come of it
but silent grieving
that now defeated we
are quietly leaving

our intimate paradise
for a noble city
where men live strangely apart
and foreign to pity.

Now once before we go
to bear their greeting
let us arrange a lone
and quiet meeting,

that in our memory
when our lives are older,
when the world has hardened us
and our hearts are colder,

we may recall how we
held azure beauty
till it was broken by
our earthly duty.

Then in our age we may
suddenly soften
and wish in our youth we had
been unwise more often.

ON A CRYSTAL VASE

The light this crystal vase reflects
on opalescent bevels breaks
prismatic, yet within directs
the bright integral gleam, and makes
the window which admits the sun
but darkling in comparison.

The source of light, if unconfined,
unconcentrated, wastes its fire:
glass, like cut crystal of the mind,
makes adamantine joy, entire
within the clarity of thought
its polished purity has wrought.

Let life then pour into the room
this mind illumines, let there be
no curtain casting casual gloom;
but guard the vase, this brilliant tree
rooted in light: it gleams—if cracked—
disintegrated, inexact.

CHILD BESIDE A TREE

The world so solemn is a place
I cannot walk by natural grace.
Though born I learn to have begun
And study how I saw the sun,
Proclaim no purpose in my mind
But that which other people find.

Yet since with real eyes I see
Not what is taught but my own tree
Growing ineffable but true,
I only play world games with you.
I speak but in the words I learn:
Thought's lock no alien key will turn.

Through this I'll grow and adult seem,
My life no longer be the dream
That grew my tree with joy for leaf
And flower of love which fruits in grief.
But from its seed in your strange land
My fate will as a sapling stand.

TRIUMPH

You praise the roses that make my garden famous,
the clarity of white, the depth of red.
I smilingly accept your commendation,
but the tulips—all that I tried to grow—are dead.

19

THE HIDDEN SPRING

There are the tears we do not see, the tears
of those who do not weep, hidden away
like crystals in dark caves, or childhood fears
of which we have no memory by day.

There are deep rivers under arid land
unknown to those who die; they downward run
full of fertility to no dry sand,
bearing their beauty to no living sun.

There are the tears we do not see, the tears
that are not wept from visible eyes, that fall
into a chasm of grief that downward sheers
to a dark land that has no life at all.

TRUTH

Ultimately there is truth only in simple statements:
in Autumn the leaves fall; I love you; we shall die.
Ultimately there is comfort only in simple actions:
the impulsive caress, laughter, the urge to cry.

Really we long to give one gift, and only
hope for a simple exchange; but man has made
his life a twisted tower, where indirectly
he wanders proudly and vainly, or cowers afraid.

There was a road to joy once, but ingeniously
we constructed a maze, forgetting to keep the plan.
Heard voices cannot be traced now: inevitably
we have established the loneliness of man.

Can you not hear, laughter to which I listen,
how in my deathly corridor I cry,
asking for simple action by simple statement,
"In Autumn the leaves fall. I love you. We shall die"?

PLAIN SPEAKING

He is the mature man. Observe him.
Like most real adults he chose a suitable friend
And made a convenient marriage, to preserve him
From love and nocturnal fear. (I recommend
That you follow suit. You'll find it best in the end.)

He was like you when young. A denial
Of early adventure would not be facing fact
(Which he taught me to do). Life is a kind of trial,
Character an achievement. To be exact,
It's a question of guided growth, pruning with tact,

Everyone his own gardener; and realisation
Of this was half the battle: early he came
To make a distinction, to have no close relation
Between ideas and life. (Thinking's a game
Really, you know—and life is not the same

As in books or discussions.) He gave up trying
To live differently—but was always a leader of thought,
Progressive and one of your sort—but as I was saying,
He lived in reality, married, made money, and bought
A house. (Now don't get restive. Really you ought

To be willing to learn, and conquer your adolescent
Dislike of the normal, that feeling you're always right.
I'm describing a pattern to follow and you mustn't
By sneering deride success and out of spite
Reject advice and experience.) In light

Of what you have said, I must correct your notion
That people can live by loving. (Let me explain.)
What you call love is just anarchic emotion—
Strong, I admit, but passing. It should be plain
That safety lies in achieving a practical, sane

And adult outlook on things. A year of marriage
Would cure you of much, for what you have to find
Is a lifetime friend to make the coffee and porridge—
Which is what he did: you'd better become resigned
To the fact that the rest wears off. You live in your mind—

That's what is wrong with you; this absurd attention
To truth and sincerity for instance. Lies
Are sometimes useful, a reasonable convention
For oiling the wheels of life (though a Christian tries,
I grant you, to keep them few, but being wise

He knows and does what succeeds). But I was portraying
This mature man, I must get back to the point.
He abandoned 'romantic' ideas. I remember him saying:
"It's facts that matter—good health, the Sunday joint,
Pride in mowing the lawn. Why, I wouldn't appoint

Myself when young to a clerkship." But he would do,
I know—he's understanding. You'd be surprised
How well he handles his men. He did all he could do
To help me when I came here. You'd be well advised
To seek his guidance. Ah, I see—you surmised

That was coming. Yes, such a man's worth knowing.
You'd like to have known him? What was that you said?
Why didn't you tell me at first—I must be going
To see his wife. What, suicide? Found dead?

THOUGHT

The oval mirror above the mantelpiece
casually distorts reflected life
behind a serene surface whose bevelled edge
colours the zero of the window's graph.

The flat field waves when my head moves, and
a red van slides on the hedge top—but now
curled in a chair to write, I find a world
changed to a still tree and half a cow.

That frayed and crinkled line is a false record
of a taut, efficient staywire. I contradict
the apparently honest error of reflection
from acquired knowledge of established fact.

But who will correct the mind's bevel
that colours the origin and plots the graph
from inadequate images and twisted data
to make what, apparently honest, we call life?

RESCUE

Spider on the log in the new fire
running in tangents and diagonals
alone with red death on a peninsula
you think a shrinking island

there is a bridge to life but you ignore it

(as those I love who helter-skelter dither
rejecting the simple explanation joining
island to island in the archipelago
of personality in the torrid sea
of human rage;

               as I
in pity building their derided bridge
of stones that used deny my passage back
to the peaceable hearth)

                  Look! I have lifted you
(as I would those) to safety. Will you forgive
this from the Firemaker?

                  (Will they?)

(in the hope that behind *me* somewhere
a machine has a god in it.)

25

WHERE WE STAND

The problem of writing is the problem of saying
clearly and accurately what we are thinking,
not have thought or will think. Words like straying
wilfully from twilight, and wander blinking

into the dazzle of other poems that say
what we think we ought to think—like a waking child
who strays from darkness into artificial day
by his mother's side in the lounge. The dream is defiled

as he tells it by the remarks of unwanted guests,
the vicar's unction or the doubting laughter
of a boffin friend of Dad's. Communion rests
on the foundation of love that follows after

the telling of truth, but in public he altered things,
and cannot be comforted now. The poet aims
not always to sound a clarion that rings,
but says words about where we stand; for nothing shames

like the pompous lie. A leaf swirls upward to fall,
and is likely later to rot. In fact, unless
the word is the thought, one had better not speak at all.
And one probably should speak only under stress;

in a single mind the rage or love will rise
like the sap in Spring to the luxury of leaf
and the fruit-creating blossom. The urgent wise
are the passionate poets we need. The destroying grief

of the age is the rhetorician with the deceitful mind
and the dumb man who knows the way but cannot speak to the blind.

THE RECKONING

Sir, I have tried, you giving me talents, love,
to help, have exalted love, have striven for friends
as no man better, have ascended above
where few walked, have gone down to ends
better undreamed, unvisited; yet I find,
had I not stirred, but sat still with a quiet mind
all would have fallen better. My striving, Sir,
to make has marred them, through my guidance they err.

Is this your parable, Sir? Did you forget
who used his talent, and lost it? Remember yet
one story unfinished, Lord. Amid my flesh
I lie as a twisted bone; oh, will the fresh
wind blow, Sir, now the charm, the talent is spent?
Or do you require of the loser alone
a recompense for the loss of the lent?

THE PARTY

Who is not here? I have invited all
who said they wished to come or whom I sought.
As they sit round the room I hear their small
insistent voices interrupting thought.

There is no vacant chair; and every kind
of conversational gambit is arranged.
Bishop and scientist, painter, brilliant mind
clatter their cups and tell why things have changed,

and what will happen, what is needed. Those
I love are here, the dark brown girl, the sage
whose bitter words fall wisely. Yet I close
the door regretfully, I search the page

of invitations for the missing name.
Who is not here? Oh whose step by the door
do I most anxiously await with shame?
Than all these one forgotten matters more.

RETURN TO EXILE

Away from the ultimate selfishness of those
whose outwardly excellent intention would make
our lives conform to a pattern they suppose
the only reality, the mind can take
a holiday in the heart's country, where peace
born of love's pain brings understanding, the clear
yet narrow domain of pity, the release
of the integral tenderness of devotion. Here
is life, and the aim of living: problems occur
only with their solution.

But can we extend
by our return the narrow country, and stir
compassion in that inhospitable land
the righteous dwell in, or understanding there?

SONNET —
TIRED OF DISORDER

Tired of disorder, I sought one who had made
A heaven of roses in neat squares of soil
Bounded by accurate paths. With careful toil
He had cleared a tangled wilderness and laid
An ordered garden, with the chequered shade
Of slender pergolas draped with the pruned coil
Climbing in perfect symmetry to foil
The blue-eyed imp who makes the priest afraid.

Vainly I sought my friend on paths that went
Beside the tended roses. He had found
Far broken walls quite overgrown with moss;
Beside a stream that murmured discontent
Naked he lay where speedwell shared the ground
With escaped nasturtiums and wild convolvulus.

II

from
WAKEFUL IN THE SLEEP OF TIME

A DANGEROUS SYMPATHY

There is nothing in this dull town to detain tourists.
I knew it too well as a smouldering twelve-year-old,
A risked reciprocity my gift and need.
Rene kissed, rampant. Dark Althea held by friendship.
In sudden shyness popular Joan bent forward
Beginningly—but her aunt came into the garden.
No drugs, no food could I offer when strike or smallpox
Quieted repetitive terraces.
                              Once without words
A fair-haired girl with light brown eyes inquired
Pale on a Sunday School windowsill, left knee raised,
Her right leg smooth by the edge.
                              She was not there again.

How then could I know what you stirred outlasted flesh?

SHIELDFIELD

Tired of polite girls richly robed
In body and conversation, I sought
A dirty slum kid whose pure need bared
In acrobatic joy white limbs she would toss
Round the high bar of the Sunday School safety fence,
Her blonde hair sweeping her toes near the rucked stone shelf
Of the pavement whose threat blasphemed like the elders' sniff
When her voice sang the laugh of her twirling belly's flash.
Every evening, except when her only dress
Was being washed, her life round death's omens raced.
Like the single star that pierces where stormclouds scud
She was for that place and for me sole light at dusk.

Except that for me, I suppose, it should have been morning
But wasn't—became night too soon, a long night
Full of day dreams in which the stilting norm
Is for all to be clothed, like their voices assuming the tone
That occasion requires—the antic, the clerical,
Leader or led, flesh cloaked, soul clad in parade
Of polite acquiescence in life as a guileful lark
For financial profit—a wardrobe of roles: to dare
To be oneself on this comic stage is obscene.
Now I awake, my dark cries naked, none knows
That it is night when offering help. I seek
God in that sordid backstreet honest kiss—
Before she earned clothes, of course. For His holy dance
I need to reclaim her between the altar candles.

NOTRE DAME DE HÉAS

I watched nine herons fly from Kinlochmoidart:
I am not there to know if they return.

Earth centred peace by sea-washed grass among mountains:
An oil platform now creates a different place.

I have heard songs in the company of girls
Sitting folded in the knees of fathers
With eyes imagining an ancient fiction
That unified mind and body in achieved grace:
Their children now have themes foreign to me.

Three hooded men did not greet me on the road to Hexham:
My car broke down near Coventina's well.
Walking among apple trees I heard no poem from Elijah
When late frost nipped the blossom.

Sages in their walled gardens tell their fame to the tulips:
My garden is rented, windswept, grows nettles, goosegrass.

I loved the marsh montbretia by a house called *Arra Venten*:
Others bought the place; I merely passed by

As now, briefly in your dark shrine, Lady of Snows,
On the way from Sauveterre to Perpignan
(Or Newcastle on Tyne to life's other city)
Travelling deviously, finding stone or flower in off-beat valleys,
I stop to admire your habit of surviving avalanches
To make here for the faithful a destination none of my journeys reach.

Help me, for them Mother of God, Queen of where they are and are go-
ing:
I return among people keen to annotate the bee trapped by the window
Not join its persistent search for air, flower, hive.

Grant me your triumph over ice falling among jagged rocks.
Be where I arrive when I've found the way.
Teach me to know why, lady of the bright snow,
You find this darkness holy.

SUNBIGGIN TARN

Gulls do not know how I think them.
They rise wheel, cry—a raucous snow storm
Over mothered nests, grey tarn, green curve
Of sheltering hollowed fell.
They do not regard themselves, they are,
Intricate, instinctive, whole in action,
Ignorantly their own in this their place.

Gulls go where they wish or die. They found
Home here. Some will return
Season after season, others fly far
Elsewhere, without nostalgia, fully where they are
Being efficiently themselves.
                              They play with the wind,
Feed on the soil's creatures, breed on ground, swim.
They are earth, air, water—in the old language
Three-fourths of the world. But they do not grieve.

This was to be my place also. I grieve
That I left. I did not live the wish or die.

Peak, round fell top, misty valley—
As far as my eyes look gulls can fly,
Live dreams of this wild land without decision,
With plover, raven, deer be part of landscape
Unknowledgeably. I decided and am elegiac.

Gorse of particular gold, remarkable orchid
Did not detain, became remembered
Not immediate.
                    It is time to go—again.

Is it only the thoughtless who are your people,
Lord, the momentary living
That make no sacrifice?

37

Do we love, only to leave; know, to lose;
Realise that place we may not be?

Earth, water, air change but remain:
Fire consumes, dies. In ashes we grieve.
Fire rekindles: Lord, this tarn,
These gulls regain identity
As to my mind first formed.

Leaving is how we grow
The pattern we become:
Grieving is how we know.

Yet restless fire,
Cannot flame's pattern stay?
Like saplings by the little nameless pool
Glimpsed as I go,
Lord, root my pentecostal tree.

LE DÉVOT CHRIST

thirteenth century woodcarving in
a chapel near Perpignan Cathedral

Your suffering, Lord, coins man's experience.
Not the sharp nails or spear but the neglect.

Men chaffered where God was, murdered in petty intrigue
When you lived to re-illuminate as now you die
Perpetually in this empty church.
                              Crowds throng
The *son et lumière* of towering Catalan altars
Rich in alleged resurection.
                    As in the world.

Seven ages ago a sculptor saw
Your swollen eyelids fall
On a lean face, ribs anguish through flesh, thin limbs
Writhe lone in fixity, nailed fast
By men's garish stupidity.
                    He is forgotten

Except that here his vision makes dead wood live
As in each age anonymous men
Are you by word or act
Till left one casual evening
Hanging solitary in the twilight of ignored pain:

God goes by on the way to His glory.

True, these deaths live—
This art, those words, that act
Unpetal to seed,
Outlast all splendid time

But, Lord, do you know?

from
THE EUROPEAN LETTERS:

II
LETTER TO BERIT[*]

PALINODE

Now, love, have done, have done.
Too soon we were apart,
just as too soon was won
my adolescent heart.

Though tides and time had flowed,
words ended, rebel thought
made memory's palinode
inevitably wrought:

Bring from Brazil the stone,
in naked onyx make
the image of your own
beauty, for beauty's sake,

so that when war has wrecked
the world in final storm,
men shall find, nude, direct,
perfection in your form.

---

*   The reader might be assisted if he recalls or looks at a reproduction of Picasso's *Guernica* and remembers why it was painted. The three preliminary poems, the first two written in 1939 and the third in 1940, may also assist.

QUESTION

In you is peace. Your footsteps' fall
quiets the wheels that tear and hurt.
Your presence brings delight to fill
empty recesses of the heart.

Stillness of mountain, plain and lake
has seemed inhuman, dead and cold,
powerless against the shades that lurk
in life defeated, dumb and killed.

You have the power to resurrect.
Have you the will, or must the grave
lie barren, while the stones restrict
even the body's power to grieve?

MEDAL

Earth vanishes, beauty fades,
but words endure,
keen as blue sharpened blades,
impeccable, pure.

Life passes, none can save
even an hour:
the stone beside the grave
outlives the flower.

Shall we engrave the dirge
that what remains
of the powerful sea surge
is the tidal stains;

or hymn the fate which takes
our lissom beauty
and hard with brilliance makes
our permanent duty?

41

LETTER TO BERIT

The northern sea
                    waves heave cold grey
isolate the posts of groynes
                    colonise
the screes in shingle
                    fluid clay
low crumbling cliff consigned to auk and fulmar
misted but edged by wind
like the town's deserted sea-wall
                    lapped obliquely
                              by the subtle swell

Severed
          the image
                    as in memory
rocks
          glaciers
                    mountains
the fjordside city with unknown people
friendly with each other
                              in alien streets
familiar streets
                    loved for your footfalls
and irresponsible since yours
                              though
not all can have that simple gaiety
                    wanton
                              with abandon
like your red hair blown
                    in my known street
                    you cycling
terror of traffic
                    charming policemen
                    acting broken English

42

The occurrence and the disappearance of ships
failing destinations beyond vague horizons
                    or in fire
                         with men howling
burning
        drowning
             The explosion of cities
                    calcination of children
Officials transforming people to skeletal statistics
Clouds hiding death that yet throbbed
                              the ears
blenched with foreboding
                    the mouth dusty in the gutter
the peculiar odour of half-vanished houses
the shape of bodies
             their blood fringing tarpaulins
             the necessity to thread that present
                              moment
Old women
        children
             finding under the stairs
                    the final stranger
recognising or beyond easing dismayed
their eyes
        the last glance
                    dark splintering rends
all fabric
Stillness after the whine crescendo
drumbeat to settling out of the air
shreds of the once alive
become dust
        around
             my own preservation of blood
                    the game
that contained me

43

                    by these waves
                              rocks
sand
        torn flesh and
                the incineration of persons
made to you
                him
                          not in
your pattern
                watchful under tyranny

                                police on the pavement
on the stair
your flesh like onyx   the offering of your
                                                          eyes
naked behind the locked door the drawn curtain
with one to you known
                    loving
                              loved
This to me
        later
                a story
like to you
        mine
                fixed in paragraphs of time
margin of detested history
recorded famous events humanly always appalling
yet lineated typeset
                the failed substitution
the honest love
                pathology of its undoing
the walk to nowhere or here
                          somewhere
                                where
apart

        peregrine
                thistledown blown chance home
hjemme
Growth rooted transient time's permitted flowers
Temporal parallels not infinite
                since
the paper runs out
                tears
                        separates
lines not even straight
                        at moments faint
                        dotted
diagrams in shelved books nobody reads
lumber burdening nocturnal janitors
And yet
the sherry party honouring you
in a hired room with two grand pianos
                jokes
                        the brief acceptance
exaggerated reality shaping the pose always
Among crowds applauding Toscanini the thin hope
you alone
        elsewhere
                a song
Casals practising Bach in an empty hall
unended conversation in a garden
the tea
        crumpets by the unnecesary fire
The taxi unshared then as ever

Because Guernica
                Dresden
                        the horse impaled
                                the woman
holding the child dead

      flames
           the thorns of the sun
knives burning in the sanctuary of rest
Seed irrecoverable
         become a field
See
      the pearl
         it has spread branches
                gnarled
wind twists the yellowing leaf

What did the child miss whom I saw
shrouded under the fallen gable
not herself
         After a count of years
she would no more have been that self
than was the sheeted corpse
What wrong committed
         what wrong to her done
pain and the road not taken
         or the road taken

arrival at the quay when the ferry outside the harbour
cleaves waves like promises
Evil is shadow beneath the lighted clock face
chimes hourly mark the festering of regret
the said
    unsaid
        the done
          omission
the peacock feather in the muddy eddy
Casals playing *Song of the Birds*
            theme of exile
              to himself
                at Prades

shutters drawn close against the glare of noon

And yet
        the cirque of cliff
                singing foam on the stones beneath
                the rowan
veins of amethyst in the sea-cave
granite
        the flight of terns
conscious warm sleep after the sowing of love
the birth of children
                playing on the sand
the severing sea
                become uniting delight
rain liquid light from red Catalan roofs
or garneting the rusty railing where
behind the droplet window a boy smiles
at the fern's diamonds in a rusty corner

Each road leads somewhere even to waste land
heather or sea-lavender
the city with eloquent cathedral
lathes turning incredible artefacts
Comfortable shoppers under the street lamps
homes glowing behind the ordered pleats of curtains
candles on the altar
                the illumination
of neonstrip over the beach
                        marram in the tidewind
mist blown over the sphagnum
                        exist each
separate
        valid
                as of right
justified even though

47

flame
      the knife in the alley
            the final stranger
in the dark beneath the empty staircase

We have met strangers on empty beaches
on crowded promenades   in sordid or elegant
                        restaurants
on marble pavements and among the droppings of
                        cattle
Once in a lane a man black-coated
tidy and soft-spoken
delighted me with anecdotes of relatives I did not
                      know of
opening a world
        mind
              gyrations of inheritance
Pages written
              and journeys yet to be recorded
long devotion to deceitful friends
thought not strangers
              limbs wrenched off
amputation of the heart
              the tread into vacuum
The integral man
              crystally single-minded
in the snake-pit of manipulators
This inures
       Those thought known
                  served
become traitors to many
             and
therefore to themselves
             Why fear the stranger
Each sleep

      each deviation
           decision at the junction
death
      resurrection again into the dying
beside new verges
          different trees
          travel
and the inn casually discovered
warm
      with wine and a dark-eyed waitress
              dimpling
Not you   that gold reddening to flame
braving a different wind
          your hair
a Moses bush
       your thighs a living onyx
in other places
       other among others
your separate page
       in another language
loved unknown grammar moving resonant words
your hours' diary
      enclyclopaedic
          unread
      yet for me
the journeys.

Commissars
     Prime Ministers
         strident voices
pompous Tartuffes
      nagging termagants
           enacted conquistadors
Economy of happiness mismanaged
worldwide

            evil painted women
invented by advertisers
                    old men
arteries scarab'd with doctrine
wreak their fantasies on Warsaw
Belfast
            the poor on valium in unheated flats
San Salvador   the slain archbishop   the
                                    martyred poor
                              as though
Belsen was not enough

Politicians invent history
                  the textbook
to avoid dogwood
                  the clouds
                        lovers in the shaded doorway
                              beneath the clocktower
Babies impaled
                  scalded
                        flayed   Weapons sold
profitably to the insane
                        for gold
to furnish Downing Street
                        the Kremlin
                              whited sepulchres
but royal carriages and May Day demonstrations
plumage preserved
                        plucked from the roasted peacock

Yet there are emeralds
                        and
perpetual faith of grass
                  Casually like pity
daffodils pierce scrap iron in the rusting yard

50

Mittenwald
      arrival triumphant   prodigal
of Norwegian campers led
by a girl sitting on a Land-Rover bonnet
you but not you
appalling sedate Germans
                   who chuntered
being en route for nowhere their journey
but yours Jugoslavia
               Greece
                  rock
                         sea
                             revolution
                                the sun
Cambridge   St. John's garden   the river
it could have been your granddaughter
lying provokingly
              except
with satisfaction eyes promised
beside and not on me
But in an Oxford garden
            a seat
                 wooden
                       green
with people passing without knowing
renunciation
        extravagant in timidity
as in all journeys
              that as in every journey
the waste   the waste   the waste

And also the triumph
to sleepwalk in search of the rose

              and wake
excited by violets
the broom
      variegated redgold
the patient exuberance of hollyhocks

What if
      seeking the White Top of Culreoch
the climb failing
           mica or quartz perpetually distant
we find
      contented
the therapy of sphagnum
not pure or absolute
that speckled quietness
You in a punt on the Cherwell
with casual acquaintances
           shall we say
affectionate
      as reported
Able to appreciate but not stand
adoration

Later
      to both
           the realisation
amid practical travel

The hands of the clock
           moved in the blackout
peopled loved
      died
in dangerous houses
flame   the sea
           Letters

by way of other countries always invaded
then silence
        fearing
the censor
        the feet on the stairs
the knock
Deliberate not being part of your difficult
                                journey
no papers to burn in Huset i Mørket
Would it be wrong now
                to mix the languages of separate travel
Who am I
                Hvem er du
Together or separate
                persons become
Vi har blatt
Though had the child lived under the gable
a cave would survive
                with amethysts
                secret
                        evocable
A book to read on another expedition
For you
        as everyone
                from you
                        as all
may compassion
                illuminate
                        with ordinary peace
your briefly unbloodstained
                        streets of snow

Now over the waters
                the fulmar broods
We recreate

                out of the chaos of accurate computers
the human
        by impressionable flesh
                fallibly divine

Before the final
                unifying
                        stranger
The clock prone in the sand
                        For seafarers
                                waves ripple
uncharted seas
                others on the voyage
                                from different
                                        journeys
to them also
                faithful

O gracious in abandon Viking
                        girl on a Land-Rover bonnet
two gardens
        the long ships

III

TWO DREAMT SEQUENCES

TWO DREAMY SEQUENCES

Variations on the Eclipse of the Unicorn (1950)
That Sufficient Gale (1979)

These two sequences—widely separated in time—resemble each other in their form and style because they are both surrealist in a way that would have been understood by André Breton. The first was dictated to me by an inner voice at the same time as I saw the pictures as on a mental screen; I did not tamper with what was dictated except to correct a grammatical confusion in ll. 13 - 15 of VI ('Unicorn'), which led me also to improve the wording. The second was different in nature in that though large sections were dictated in the same way, some others were composed (unconsciously in the dictated style) to describe what was being shown on the mental screen. In no instance was the whole poem composed and I had no idea what was going to happen in the story until I saw it occur.

I say this because there are certain philosophical or pychological concepts implied in the poems—but I did not plan these or think them out. Even sententia were dictated and not the result of any conscious or logical thought. After the event I can see, in fact, on what some of the landscapes are based and at times what incidents were reflected (though not narrated), but it would be tedious to write geographical, mythological or autobiographical notes (though Twelve Men's Moor does exist as remembered—in East Cornwall).

In the middle of a prosaic lunch I heard a voice distinctly say, "The dwellers in eternity communicate in simple symbols with the travellers through time." *They may: or these sequences may present critics and psychologists with a wild-goose-chase I hope they find enthralling.*

B.M.H.

For those interested, ll. 13 - 15 of 'Unicorn' originally read:
        once more a god, who changed (all that he dare)
        her to a tree and him a waterfall
        because she loved him, yet she could not bear

        the terror of his being real at all

VARIATIONS ON THE
ECLIPSE OF THE UNICORN

I   PASSAGE BEYOND THE ADULT

Because the childhood soldiers on the floor,
bed-feather plumed, fell down in rows to win
the lady's fortress by the cupboard door;

and since the pencilled story in the thin
green notebook had the satisfactory word
on the last page, this man is to begin

the passage back and forward in the absurd
real corridor whose clarity of light
dazzles with truth, from which, once he has heard

the flute-like voices from the windowed height
tell unmistakable fact, he must emerge
into day's darkness. In that brilliant night

he saw life first and clear, and now the urge
comes to explain to those who blindly see
unreal shapes dreamed true, who in the surge

of death's denial cry he cannot be.

May 4th 1950

57

II   ECLIPSE OF THE MOON

Because the unicorn had recognised
her wanton innocence, and placed his gift
too gently for her heart to be surprised,

her lucid thoughts were rippled in a swift
river of laughter over russet stones,
clear like her eyes, but in an eddied drift

his effort stirred, and nothing now atones
for the lost light his hoofs obscured to cross
the ford for her sake; yet her dumb heart owns,

now he has fled, the too lamented loss
is of one sullied moment in a stream
which was his gift and barrier: a toss

of water backward hid a crystal gleam
that was there all the time, and reappeared
when he had gone; and she will live that dream

he offered her, without him, as he feared.

                                        May 25th 1950

III   BREAKER AT NEW MOON

The wave had risen where the wide-winged bird
flew from land like a white thought that beat
in dream's blue circle when Endymion heard

climbing the stairs of sleep Selene's feet.
Unconsciously the Psyche of the sea
stirred to this form when Eros like a fleet

58

bodiless wind had blown invisibly,
seeking in her too lonely birth to make
that lovely crest in which he came to be.

But fleeing from the breath that made her take
so willingly the graceful form she bore,
turning her head of foam to watch the wake—

which was her sight of him—upon the shore
he had foreseen she ignorantly broke
his love her body, and the pebbles tore

life to the swirl he saw when he awoke.

May 27th 1950

IV   METAMORPHOSES OF THE UNICORN

It moved so gently through the golden field
that the bird stayed and sang behind the grass
pure notes that flickered sunlight on the sealed

buds of the flowers that waved to see it pass.
But no one watched beside the stream which thought
its momentary image, like the glass

flashing the secret wish to her who caught
a chance reflection as she shyly moved
naked across the bedroom. Yet it fought

Narcissus-like for life when it had proved
beauty a right to live: a brutal hound,
now that it was, pursued it till it grooved

59

stark grief upon the inoffensive ground,
behaving so unlike itself it ceased
to be, and unbelieving men who found

the deathmark said it was a savage beast.

May 27th 1950

V   PASSAGE THROUGH REALITY

Because the fabled horn was thought to cure
the madness in the real heart, they urged
that she should wait beside the spring whose pure

blue water mirrored her dark hair, submerged
like nereid foliage near her shaded face
echoing the rock by which the pool was verged.

So half asleep she felt her fingers trace
the rippled outline of herself, until
she dreamed him into being. Yet the pace

of that swift flight from those who sought to kill
shattered his imaged form beside her own:
awake she saw escape beyond the hill

the real beauty she had never known
out of that dream. She thought the men had said
they would not harm him, yet she heard the groan

with which he vanished when they found her dead.

May 27th 1950

VI   APOTHEOSIS OF THE UNICORN AS PAN

Because her flowering stillness on the lawn
stirred the too lustful god to chaste surprise,
he came to her as quiet as a fawn,

tender as raindrops, gentle as the rise
and fall of water in an inland pool
that hidden streams make tidal: and her eyes,

catching the timid glance, turned to the cool
moss by the shading trees, and wished to flow
pure like a stream, from which, a legend's fool,

he would but pluck one reed. She did not know
the sadness of that melody, and care
to save her from that knowledge made him grow

once more a god: she stood transmuted there,
a tree beside a ceaseless waterfall,
for she had loved him but she could not bear

the terror of his being real at all.

                                        June 17th 1950

VII   Epilogue: DA CAPO

Because like Deianira both will trust
the Nessus deathwish, and, too innocent,
he hope to be and she suspect as lust

what makes his being pure, nothing is meant
by their experience but a tapestry
that re-enacts the myths. The maiden went

61

to wait beside the spring; he came to be;
but Eros and Endymion awoke;
he vanished and she died. This summary

is all that can be made, for Syrinx broke
in those too passionate hands, and Pan became
beauty in waste of water. Curls of smoke

form what is seen of an eternal flame.
Others will pity what they cannot alter,
the pattern that will always be the same:

turn how we may, no oracle will falter.

June 17th 1950

THAT SUFFICIENT GALE

I   LETTER TO ARIADNE

To face Hell's maze was my resolve, I know
though I'd no Thesean power or Orphean charm.
You spun the thread that gave me heart to go.

Armed with my naked self I quelled alarm
and found the Minotaur a gentle beast,
the Dismal King forgiving, but a storm

pelted with hail not Hades but the crest
above the cave-mouth where the labyrinth
emerged to daylight earth. It was the best

thing, I suppose, for her I'd led, to seek
shelter by going back—and you were right
to leave the bobbin where you'd knew I'd look,

and leave without thrones,islands and all that,
happily somewhere Bacchus needn't wander
and maenads leave in peace. Myths make a rut

you needn't ride your bike in. But I ponder
how to get through to you (from the rocky shelf
I'm now alone on, having no lyre, no thread,

no path to where your happy streams meander)
the truth I nearly died for; so I tread
sharp flints again, armed with my naked self.

26–27th April 1979

63

II   BEYOND THE STACKYARD

There was a desolation no one saw
for no one went: a sluggish rivulet
got lost in mud, dumped stones and sodden straw

near twisted barkless trees. Concrete had set
in strange unnatural shapes where bags had burst
in winter rains; old manure formed a mat

treacherously imitating grass. A blest
oasis pond circled by willows shone
unreachable within that sordid waste.

And yet a wharf, a flat-topped wall began
to bridge the void, inviting me to go;
the end sloped gently down to filth unknown

since hidden by nettles, goosegrass, dock. I knew
poisonous chemicals mixed with earth so rich
it grasped like quicksand. By the willows, though,

there bloomed the rose that had long obsessed my dreams.
It might root nowhere but beyond that ditch
where warring effluents plaited lurid streams.

28th April 1979

III   THE PROMISE

The house faced sunrise and the fields of dawn—
varied counterchange of bright corn and shade,
dark lamps of woods whose brown wicks edged to green.

Windows and doors welcomed the Spring inside
as guest to patterned rooms reflecting grace,

exchanging flower for flower, for all relied

on birth as pledge, believed that love would trace
perpetual mobiles on the lighted wall
as day moved through the branches. Once, blown loose,
the nurtured broom tapped on the pane, and grass
between the docile roses teased neat soil.

But nothing forecast that sufficient gale
which shattered glass and roof, laid rafters bare
and stirred the kind hearth to consume the whole.

Now an old tramp cowers from dawn's blizzard where
bulbed snakes of fungus eat the nursery floor.

8 – 10th May 1979

IV   GENESIS REFOUND

Hidden within the derelict garden behind
thistles, nettles, dock, the broom grows gnarled
and mossy like an apple tree, entwined
half way by bramble and wilding rose.

                         A cold
dank mildew slides on broken paving stones
making their lunacy real. Shadows enfold
the thwarted sundial: time is proclaimed by bones
of rabbit, weasel, heron. Stream and pond
that sang and coruscated here form dry
receptacles for leafmould. Spring has found
its satanic reflex, non-Eden.

                      Yet, from sky
that seems a colour echo of the ground

65

one sudden shaft of light illuminates

one twig of a peeling branch shouting the flowers
harlequin red and yellow.

                    Fence and gates
firmed with barbed wire, rusted and strong, have kept
nature's reversion true and what endures
defeats design, destroys the measured hours,
mocking our wisdom makes no symbol apt.

                                        24th May 1979

V   COASTLINE

Within the field she lies: flowered grass
powders and dapples naked limbs
sleep ignorantly wantons. Trees

prune wind of roughness. Skylark homes
unfrightened near her bed. For hours
she could wait there and hares make forms
as natural as the anthers her breath stirs.

Beside the field he straddles a high branch
to gaze past dunes to sea round scars
of glistening rock. Hopes launch

flotillas of his dream. But what,
if he looks down, will staunch
a wound immediate
to both? His eyes leave shores
she earths on. She is not
who lay there if she wakes
nor will he tell his vision if he speaks.

66

VI   CHIVALRY

It was the monster seeking to be kind
undid the knight, who temperately fought
and dropped defence when his opponent, blind
with fury and blood, charged the containing wall,
turned suddenly and clawed him from behind—
then said that love was all that she had sought.

So they released the maiden to the thrall
she'd loved while bound, and both were made to serve
the festive tables in the candled hall.
It must be said she did not mind at all:
she kissed the knight for saving her but thought
life with that wild boy happy when they fled—
yet found his freedom cast her as a slave.

Since she was kind the monster stripped the knight
of armour, weapons, tent and maps. His horse
would draw their carriage when they gently rode
within the park, for it was such delight
to have one's world and never stray outside.

The end came rapidly: the monster's curse
grew passionately loving when the maid
penniless, lone, asked shelter while she bore
her grief's first son. Claws lit the welcoming fire
in which at dawn child, knight and girl lay dead.

25th May 1979

VII   POINT OF DEPARTURE

Set on a parabolic hill the town
beckoned the traveller with its promised care

but the road ran first through floods, all bridges down,

and when it climbed the gorge like a winding stair
landings had been eroded by torrent and ice:
lorries, cars, coaches had turned and fallen sheer
to forested rock; silent, wheels in the air,
they entombed worker and tourist in a place
where rust and decay would feed luxuriant trees.

Yet clambering on through days and nights when ease
was memory or hope he reached the gate
which opened as he came. No watchman rose
from the polished bench to greet him, no one met
him graciously in the deserted street.
All palaces seemed his but no one sat
at dining-tables; in arrased galleries
chairs were arranged, portraits on every screen,
urbanely motionless with haunted eyes,
mocked frenzied search—no servant could be seen,
no marquis, châtelaine or dark-eyed maid.
Even each small house waited—aired, warm, clean—
some monumental nothingness.

                           He fled
through alley and lane to where a ruined broch,
low lintel garnet-studded, gloomed apart
echoing its rock, its past. There rats gnawed bones,
found bread in crannies. Looking from the gap
where stone stairs ended he gazed over a loch
on which a man and woman rowed, each stroke
united in rhythmic voyage to a makeshift port
where burning thatch patterned the sky with smoke.
He heard the water below him gently lap
his boat, oars ready.
                    Had he strength to start?

3rd June 1979

VIII   ISLANDS

They had set out as hardy friends to sail
through all known seas and found reliance firm.
Now two survived wrecked on this sandy isle,
before then undiscovered. Faith in storm
to create faith had justified at first:
one could weave tents of branches, one reform
a desolation to a sense of home,
harvest productive gardens. What was lost?
They could live bravely and record their tale—
later be fêted, famous.

                              Day and night
made month and year, and the recurrent frost
and rhythmic heat brought nothing that would change
themselves or where they were. Each week they wrote
less in that epic diary. The hinge
between their minds rusted. Each walked alone
more often; each recalled streets unknown
to the other, then dreamed the girls had died,
the houses rotted—and screamed or wept. So when
rescuers came one body lay to the west
with blood-soaked wrists. On the beach to the east
no one could tell why the second man had spread
patterns of shells to frame his final bed.

                                        10th June 1979

IX   PILGRIMAGE

To reach the God who wrote, "*Sell all you have
and climb this apparently impossible height
which you will master through the strength of love*"

he tore his limbs on sharp set stones while light

69

smote vision just this side of blindness, crawled
wormlike through mud in darkness, slept remote,
exhausted, lone, on rotting leaves that mould
fouled sickeningly though it gave all he could eat—

until, at the end, he found a path through cold
pure crystal that seemed the symbol of his gain.

Knowing the road was right, in faith that held
all courage firm he strode to a high plain
and found the marble city. To quell pride
he swept its streets to win the price of bread,
the cost of clothes and—ready at last—made known
his wish for audience, entered with head bowed,
hallowing the jewelled floor, and raised his eyes
in hope to Him he wished to serve. The God
looked down and smiled. *"Oh, you have come,"* He said
in that enthralling voice men long to hear;
"Some who came earlier are still unemployed.
Sorry I wrote—don't need you any more."

21 – 23rd June 1979

X   THE SAVIOUR

He was abandoned on the beach, alone
by men who sailed away to search for gold
on other islands. This, they thought, had been
explored before—a little field, once tilled,
had broken fences near a ruined hut.
Tradition made them leave, of course, a case
of lemonade, tinned food and books they thought
might while away the time till he was killed
by natives, nature or himself. His views

of where and what to seek had caused, they said,
the expedition's failure.
                        He repaired
the walls, the roof, the fences with a speed
and energy that proved him still inspired
to strive to satisfy for all the need
that caused the whole adventure. And he found
gushing from a cave of amethysts a stream
that clothed its banks with golden filigree
of nourishing plants, elixir of a dream.
His notes in bottles drifted far, and land
so rich as this brought hordes of profiteers
who quarrelled about the ownership of sea
which though not mapped all claimed as always theirs,
while they trod his flesh and bones in the gilded sand.

                                        8th July 1979

XI   DECEMBER GIRL

She dreamed she was a garden climbing a hill
from tropical valley to the clouded snow,
terraced between slopes—and perpetual
in that, somewhere in her, seed sown anew
opened to life unseen while further down
young leaves uncurled or golden harvest grew
glossed straw that bore germens and food as crown.

Men walked on paths within her being, smoothed
pastures of her identity and hid
thought in her woods where winds through branches breathed
the restlessness of sentient peace. Some god
or faun strayed irresponsibly among the brown

71

ferns or green grass and flowers blue, yellow and red—
yet was for all that lived saviour and guide.

Waking she felt that genius wilt: between
the angry winter curtains swords of light
flashed anger at her vision, but she knew
he would return because he safely fled.

Through threatening day both crop and blossom fade
but on the copse and hillocks of the night
dew freshens what will rhythmically grow
by tidal dominion of the ascendant moon.

16thJuly 1979

XII   BEDROCK

Beside the entrance to the abandoned mine
he passed a shack where no one seemed to live—
rotting leaves roofed cracked walls of crumbling stone.
He had come far, with guides at great expense,
convinced he would find diamonds, to save
a country's fortune and create his own.
Now, though, he'd little left, enough to give
a fortnight's wages—but no recompense
for the trust of three who had helped him to survive.
All would depend on what they found.

In faith
they used their last explosives to prepare
a passage for him and his three friends to explore.
When he returned dazed, bleeding and alone
the others knew as fact what had lurked as fear.
Sourly they took their money and had gone

72

before his mind cleared like the tunnelled maze
where head held high in hope struck jagged truth.

He tottered to the shack to rest. He found
inside writhed a haggard girl clasping the hand
of a stinking corpse. She begged with twisting eyes,
fouled limbs and feverish sweat. He cleaned the ground
and made a bed of straw and fern. He lay
holding her life there after he had brought
water and food from what supplies were left
and covered a grave with rocks.
                                                Through night and day
he held and washed and tended a stricken brute,
in moments finding grain grown wild and fruit
from derelict gardens—till those eyes grew bright
with sane response as briefly mists would lift
from human mountains also.
                                                A child from play
ran home one evening to a settled farm
bringing from forbidden rocks in ignorant joy
five rubies unclenched by rats near a skeleton arm.

Was it courage or doubt to tread them in dimming clay?

                                                27th July 1979

XIII   VOYAGE

The day came when no golden oriole
flew to the treasured branch, some leaves edged brown,
rain pierced the forest roof, the glade, grown chill,
offered no haven from the glaring sun
nor, when that weakened, hid from the sharp wind.
Time agonised again this haunt of man

from which, now wings were silent, nymphs had gone—
he was not what they sought there but had joined
in someone else's dream and since they knew
the seasons of that land he slept alone.

There seemed no choice but travel and he found
an old white horse trapped in a thistled field
outside the trees. He could unlatch the gate
and follow that tired head south where swallows flew
high over him towards their change of world.
Their instinct made them leave him by the sea
while the bright-eyed horse ran to others through a marsh pool
among tides of grassy sand. It seemed his fate
to have as guide what knew the way to where
he could not rest or could not reach.

                                    A boat
he idly ignored came drifting to the shore
as he threw shells at dwindled ripples. Then air
exploded in fire, earth shook, spirals of spray,
stones, mud and brine hurled havoc till he fled.
But the tossed boat reached him cowering in fear
by a bush that flamed on a sanddune, safe but not
sheltered—and in it lay a sunscorched girl
asleep or dead. He clambered aboard, to guard
her body from spumeblown pebbles and driving hail.

How long gales swept them he never knew, but woke
with her in a place of rocks. He could not steer
except with raw arms and hands, but somehow moved
that weak boat, inspired by distant trees and smoke,
to a blue harbour curved among quartz-glints and tropic sand.

Men greeted him with gratitude, revived
the girl they'd lost and restored her to her home,

to husband, child and hearth. They said he had come
as king because pilgrim and saviour. To understand
was denied but he could accept.

                    As moonlight broke
the torment of his bed he rose to find
on a memoried branch that now glowed evergreen
swallows and orioles calmly waited dawn.
                              31 July — 1 August 1979

XIV   THE RIVER

Headstreams eroded peat, babbled their hope
detecting gravel where curlew bubbled clear
all through long Spring. He verified the map
and the primal runnel washed a piece of spar
blue-veined and opalescent. A talisman
of similar rock lay by it. However far,
he determined to take it where the river ran
from plateau through valley with round hills to the sea—
though old and tired. His mad resolve began
although he did not know why he should care
or what the reality of his aim could be.

There was no path. Roads bridged the river and led
to town or village where shelter was, a bed
could be hired or begged, but he stumbled on through scree
from disused quarry or mine till he found a stair
moss-cracked but dropping to an abandoned quay.
Beyond, the river widened, curved and spread
among lush woods and the pastured breasts of hills.
He had almost found his end, for a viaduct
towered in far distance, whole when his map was made

75

and majestic still, though one arch broke derelict.
He knew that a mile from that, the estuary
opened to sand and tide. But waterfalls
down rocks now blocked his way where the desolate wharf
met wall and cliff. The time had come to wait
and sleep.

He did not know who dreamed the boat
and, since the girl rowed so well, did not expect
she would juggle with the stone as she danced in the wakeful surf.

4 – 5th August 1979

XV   DESTINATION

In mist and gale, the wind not thinning the mist
but thickening fleeting sections, creating hope
of clear light that fled or vanished, he knew he must
press on from cairn to cairn, the track so steep
that each mark discerned was glimpsed then lost except
for faith and tortured memory, but to grope
round boulders and over cutting edges kept
the spirit active and knifed the flesh from sleep.
He knew too that near his side the rockface dropped
sheer beyond cornice of snowy grass and ice
the treacherous year had woven and polished. Stopped
by a frozen step he dreaded that precipice—
but briefly—then hauled his body over an edge
to find the land grew gentler; snow lined the course
of the path and stream beside it. The summit ridge
gloomed and was gone. But, this direction seen,
his way was known. Soon he redeemed his pledge
to quixotic folly and stood tired and alone
where they said he could not reach. Wind cleared the sky

suddenly: on the plateau the sun shone
so that he saw the desolation there—
the ruined mine, the abandoned gold, the store
of useless engines, and a derelict tower
that other fools had built and not known why.

The gale resumed, mist hurtled round, obscured
the grief, and re-established the need to try
in shelter to solve the mystery he had feared
would await him there. Inside a shack he found
a table laid—bread, wine—and a clean bed lured
his aching body. But groaning on the ground
his hostess writhed, an aged woman gnarled
and horrible. He did what had been planned.
They ate and slept, not knowing if the curled
limbs that enfolded warm would ever turn
to fabled youth. Outside night swirled or prowled
till over the far ridge dawned the omniscient moon.

26th August 1979

XVI   AGAINST CALUMNIATING TIME
(Troilus and Cressida III, iii, 145 et seq.)

They met again when old. When young they had parted
pledged, but their contexts changed, so that one grieved,
one, thwarted, grew hastily angry. Together, whole-hearted,
they would have been one paragraph in the many-leaved
bible of passion and peace. Forgetting each other
they were different stories. She was a woman who moved
with wanton grace that brought enemies together
in drawing-rooms sweating violence through the polish

77

hidden by flower-arrangements: husband and mother
changed title-deeds to footnotes to abolish
the record of possessive demons, and damp-courses
sweetened cellars and bedrooms. His baroque pages
enlightened dark alleys of minds and nations: forces
flowered from pitheaps and sewers; men dreamed new ages
of tranquil joy, but reaching forwards fell—
and blamed. She too was ignored as the subtle orgies
of established corruption rotted the parchment, a scrawl
of trivia blotted the palimpsest, poisoned sources
that might have confirmed the blossom. Now, when all
their deeds were "alms for oblivion" they stood
embarrassed in a hotel lounge. In each a voice
wept lyrics as they smiled, for neither could
explain why they did not normally rejoice
at the comedy end. But the past determined choice
to die, grieve fresh, or illuminate on a bed
in wheaten gold what youth might have scribbed red.

28 – 31 August 1979

XVII   LEGEND

To form the path they dammed the swamp and made
three sluices to create a trickling stream.
The marsh became a pond where children played
with toy boats; swans adopted it as home
and fish that bred in little feeding brooks
swam among weeds like light in a green shade.

The swamp became a legend like the lakes
that once had filled the valley among far hills
where now sheep grazed. Cattle found the old bed
of a storybook river had sweet herbs that rills

which murmured there made succulent. Only the dead
who lay forgotten in bracken between high rocks
beside a ruined tower could have told the end.

Men think the world as décor for their dream:
its scenes are transitory but not as planned.
Depths behind springs await the cyclic storm;
torrents break bodies of agonised children drowned
in treacherous parkland ignorant of doom.

6 – 7th September 1979

XVIII   MEMORY OF TWELVE MEN'S MOOR

There was a path he did not take. It tracked
by the Withey Brook to reach a granite house
set clean among lush fields. Though its bed was flecked
with glistening mica, brambles obscured its course
marred by spring thorns, and since he did not know
the people there, he turned by a flowering gorse
and climbed the moor to the eerie hill of Stowe
where caves had sheltered hermits and a wind-hewn crag
dripped near parched rocks and strange eroded shapes
whose precarious balance eluded time. A crow
lumbered away. He saw behind through gaps
in pillars the weathered circles of magic stones
and memorials of ancient kings. The drag
of myth pulled his spirit back. Wind creaked his bones
and froze flesh-seeking arms, but he stumbled on
to the eastern breast. In the gale's teeth he stood
to see the bright world stretch far, the rivers run
through wooden valleys with little bridges—glad
fertile hills tempted. And thus his course began
to explore, enjoy, suffer, report. He fled

into adventure:

But now, far off, alone
in a distant but similar country, wished to return:
that path he ignored, where did it lead, and who
waited within that remembered house? He knew
that like his journeyed self all would have grown
through mutability to a different place—
new sedge would mark the brook—and those paths could trace
deceptive patterns through bogs, and the traveller, lost
after mist and storm sleep lonely till he died;
though in that dream what guide would guess he found
a skeleton cleaned upon the acid ground
would prove the inevitability of peace?
Search triumphs in sight of the abandoned house,
the vision within immortalising mind.

14th September 1979

XIX   VARIATIONS FOR TROILUS AS PRINCE OF TYRE

What did the Maenads tear, body or soul?
Did they unwrap a parcel for the world,
cast pearls on ferrying waters? And what role
did Ariadne play while Theseus hurled
his power about the kingdoms? It is Roman
to call Dionysus Bacchus (easily swirled
are drunken maids in oil on canvas); women
may populate deserted islands, root
deeper than Naxos vines. The myths are common
to shallow psychologists and those who meet
Magdalens maligned in gardens being true.
Not every skin-stain blemishes the fruit.
Who guesses what Eurydice can know

80

because her Orpheus lost his faith? The flame
forgotten by vestals may burn brighter so.
New variations on the tragic theme
change mood but justify the human flow.
Lear's defeat and triumph are the same.

21st September 1979

XX POSTSCRIPT TO ARIADNE

I am my labyrinth and you have given
the thread to lead me to that outside maze
I also search. A substitute for heaven
you had no right or power to give, and ways
to alter the geology of both
do not exist: we have to accept each phase
of world beyond our fathoming, and truth
is what kicks us as there—and what we dream
when honest imagination finds its myth
ruthless, unsentimental and no home
for fantasy denying what's perceived
and felt. There is a central room
that once the human thread has been received
willingly and not tangled grants us free
entry and exit. Nothing is removed
from either maze; no barrier can be
holed or demolished; and the minotaur
is always what it is though we may see
it wasn't what was fabled. Other lore
needs adding to the stock—that is our task
in separate lives. I cannot think we're here
to enjoy unstruggling and it's mad to ask
to avoid the legend or simply re-enact
the tragedy of the blind. We live in dusk,
not night or day, must love the inexact
since all we see is what our eyes reflect.

I'll meet you where realities intersect—
root, stem, flower, seed, not merely scent of musk

21st September 1979.

IV

FIVE MEDITATIONS

I — VARIATIONS ON MAURICE DE VLAMINCK'S LA RIVIÈRE NORMANDE*

I

Trees may seem still but live sap hidden flows,
branches have snapped, trunks twisted, bent to withstand
gales after summer heat. That blue-roofed house
has moved and settled till its white walls strained
away from true; their even brightness browned.

The river's movement powerfully reflects
green bank, arched bridge, sky's purple threat too near
that red roof's passion, dimmed as it reacts
with the gable's outstanding white, whose naive glare
yet doubts the river's answer, because, obscure,

the other verge muddies blue-green beneath
a funeral building that towers anonymous.
Not firm but its formless self, deceptively smooth,
the river feeds and erodes tree, bank and house.
Earth is chaos in vertigo finding peace,
orgasmic identities in a quiet place.

---

* In variation VIII reference is made to two other paintings — *Les Chaumières* and *Sentier par le Village*.

85

II

Forms merge, exist
each with identity
but water's lust
to echo blurs their boundary.

Image declines
each chance to photograph,
bends and browns lines,
recolours walls, smooths what was rough.

We think we know
which house is fact, which dream,
but gaze can go
inside the echo, not the room.
Here more than rivers flow.

III

We are used to reflections being imprecise
and know that the river moves
but having also to presume that trees
root in green darkness deprives
the perceptive mind
of the comfort of its own ground.

IV

There is no one on the bridge, no face
at any window. Men are here
to build, lop, colour. The place
like the river reflects a creation unclear
in water and not stable in air.

V

The river is the theme where what seems firm
reverberates its instability:
the house was built to withstand, trees attained form,
the bridge connected separates: yet, see—

the bank flows downwards to the stream, or hangs
over the water; in interstices
chaos whirls or seeks shape; what's sordid springs
seeming to love air, cloud and distances.
Eye cannot tell what's hill or sky, what flings
shadow or light with no assuring cause.

Blake achieved wiry bounding lines;
here things have edges that
fly up or blur. The pines
merge, roofs dissolve, reflections meet

their imprecise reality. The mind
knows less as it perceives
more, and the dark we find
in ragged stillness moves.

VII

That blue-roofed house is the church.
Involved in atmosphere we failed till now
to recognise the apse which seems detached
from the rest, threatened. Behind that wall
we imagine petition by candle, red flicker of faith;
but though we need, when we feel the universal whirl,
to light our prayer, we do not know the truth
about what goes on beyond wall and river's flow.

VIII

The river precedes the men who built
the house, focused the church, bridged between,
the grass happened on the bank silt
and each tree's form is its own.

Parallels, joined lines, echoed shapes
are planned, casually relate, or clash and cut,
but together image life—the hopes
that open, despairs that shut.

I think of two thatched cottages each with a tree.
Four share the savage sky and that atmospheric white
striking through limbs and edges. We see
earth's ragged claws grasp light.

Or the lane through the village, that relates
(from the dark) red roofs, white walls to the arrow of dust
that past black fence, vague field, tormented tree
points to what mystery,
what twisting lights,
material lust?

IX

To me my mind is a house, to you it reflects
in the stream of living; you think,
feel, speak—my love constructs
trees, houses, bridge, or water where they sink.

Your walls' light fingers strum
on the zither of my river
not knowing the urge of the stream,
weeds, eddies, fish, mud water glosses over.

Bridge me, strengthen both banks, so that we
are house, church, stream, and tree—
earth's tower of sap enclosing sky.
Reflections play variations but need not lie.

X

Images
inspirations
agonies

form and
unform
unmake
and make

separate they
materially
relate

II — MESLAND: A WINTER'S TALE
FOR THE HEATH OF A HORNED GOD

Mesland means Hermes moor, but Hermes
is Cernunnos Latinised and beside the altar
has become a saint along with Sylvain the wood-god.
The romanesque arch of the church porch
has twenty-six bearded heads and a capital
of the central doorway a horned Ammon of Thebes
who in a mythology of death was ithyphallic,
husband of his mother, making earth fertile.

I found this out afterwards. I went to Mesland
by accident, on the way through Onzain to Chaumont
seeking the Loire and the château of Madam de Staël;
These I found, but Mesland found me.
More than 'found'—it enthralled for no known reason.
That is how true myths work, they are there
as an ambiance to trap you, before the guide books,
the archaeologists and fabricators of legend-kits
display their wares; and that is why
the rational behaviour-cult is to be derided:
its derision assumes research invented a pseudo-
inspiration, but epiphany precedes wisdom.
(On the journey the three magi were probably as foolish
as their modern counterparts, designers of knowledge
in limited schemes, though the wide-ranging gods,
who do not need theology, wait beside that stream
or among bushes that seem random on the mountain slopes.)

The guide books will tell you of 'Merlin's land'
because by night the prettiest girls in the village
would run to ring the church-bells (barefoot, reefing their nightgowns)
and send threatening storms to drown Onzain, so saving
their vines nourished by granitic sand over tufa
with grapes ripened by the sun on reflecting pebbles
that also kept water where it should be—in the soil.
I am bewitched by the 'sorciers de Mesland'

(sorceresses apparently, though I did not meet one)
not in the fairytale sense, but somehow
because of that brook, the bridge, those bushes,
and *le Prieuré*, to which I returned
later, as to a home-coming, to buy wine.

There is something remarkable in a field of sunflowers
that you cannot photograph—a profusion of surprise,
a livingness of search and response, a moving glory.
I saw a German trying to snap it, standing on his car roof
to get the whole view not blocked by the edge,
the perspective of the sun's vision, but you cannot arrest
and fix by however marvellous a technology
what is of light and air and the earth transformed
naturally into echoing colour to praise the star
that however small comparatively is for us
the source of being, generator, to whom
we turn as *tournesols*, seek like the flower
which has become—as wine has become its father
and through stem, blossom, fruit and fermentation
also its mother. That is how Mesland became
and what I am and why these fields, these vineyards
seem trees with the sap of symbol, not the formal
pattern, academic, stylised, categorised rigid.

I do not mind if Our Lady of Einsiedeln
is Isis or Mary—she is what she is—
or if the peasants of Héas carved a goddess in wood,
buried her and said they found her. She survived storms,
remaining intact through hurtling ice and stone
as we all want to do. Mary of Magdala
complained of the legal rigidity of Peter
(who was rebuked by Matthew for anti-feminism—
'Whom the Saviour made worthy, who are we to reject?')
(It is worthwhile enquiring why some gospels are apocryphal:

it is not merely a forged text but unfitting stories
involving heretical thought, compassionate flesh.)

The history of Mesland is probably like that
of other villages—love, rape, murder, forgiveness,
hatred and the reconciliation, resistance and collaboration—
but it became what it is now and was for me
—somehow beyond comprehending, an appeal,
a sanctification, a memory of what was not known
until I remembered it. There is nothing 'magical'
in real magic; it requires no conjuror
and is its own medium, like these words
that occur to me, as wine occurs, through growth
of the grape, its bruising, fermenting, maturing
as something essentialised and intoxicating:
'Appellation TOURAINE-MESLAND Controlée'.
It would be the same though, even if not 'controlled';
good laws are of recognition but not imposed,
as sunflower and vine may be tended but not manufactured.
We eat and drink the pebble, the leaf, the brook:
crumbled soil and hot sun flesh the soul with light.
It is not belief, but faith, hope, love that survive,
like granite in clay, resilient stones in the stream.
What matters is *ce qui demeure*—what remains, dwells:
Anatole France, sardonic reductionist, 'cynic',
detesting whatever brought human suffering,
loved Black Virgins and whores who became saints.
With Balzac he shares Saint-Cyr, further down the river,
and thought the sixteenth-century statue of St Anne
teaching Mary to read enshrined a valley's wisdom.

That is at Germigny-des-Prés, appropriately nearer the source
of this uniting Loire—but now I want to know
what is the origin of Dame-Marie-les-Bois

on my twisting route back to Saint-Ouen-Les-Vignes,
where I stayed a lifetime of two days and nights.

I have danced a twilight's eternity in the home paddock of God.

My mind strays, as I did, past the church of Saint Ouen ...
I cannot (now) hear the crickets but I'm told they sing
till the evening fills with their joy. I can hear the distant click
of *boules* on the sand beside the still water,
not Jordan but the Ramberge, which little dams temper
in its flow to the Cisse, which merges with the Loire,
like the Indre, the Cher and Châtillon's *ancien canal*,
which seeks, as sanity should, union at Saint-Aignan.

III — AMSTERDAM SUITE

I   PEREGRINATION AT VARIED PACE

Unparabling city, built on sand or on wood in water!
There are no rocks. Builders imported stone
or exotic marble but mainly created brick.
Gales and tides, like man's subtle or overt assault,
have beaten or gnawed this artefact, which withstood them
to become now openly friendly, with secret places,
so rooms where Jews hid or closet Catholics prayed
are exhibited now like expiatory candles,
as the whores wait not quite naked in their windows or two
                                                      coarse nymphets,
semi-punk, denim'd, jewelled with chains and padlock,
beg in the opulent street near the Stock Exchange
on whose steps the bearded guitarist slept at noon
while the street organ blasted his pitch. This is the place
where nothing human is alien—women of every colour,
darkly pretty or neon blonde, men portly or leanly young
abundantly accept, washed in waterclear light,
each moment's random vividness: non-selective Thélème—
Do what you will—but *Remember O thou Man,*
O thou Man, O thou Man, Remember O thou Man,
sing the towers, *Thy time is spent*—yet at least can have known
variegations like the lights of Damrak or the shops of Kalverstraat,
near which (Sex by Access or Visa) the Begijnhof
encloses decorous houses and two churches in a square
of grass and blue flowers. *Boykot Shell, Americans*
Out of Everywhere (though plenty are here!) or incomprehensible
symbols blotch ancient walls or shout from so high up,
did monkeys contort with paintsticks or the city fathers
conveniently leave scaffolding? Yet this is order:
a compact city, as mapped from the air,
with canals in semicircles appropriate to the lost
who stroll till they find themselves—and learn there are four
main types of gable but all have hooks for pulleys
so you can hoist in whatever you want—Cleopatra

in a carpet if she dislikes stairs, though adult elephants
might wedge in the window—yet both would be welcome;
for the shipwrecked built a Dam to save from sea and river
where the square is now royal and plebeian, so that
beyond the pigeons a lone old man can sit
playing a trumpet (rather well) to himself
or to the world, for him possibly the same:
both know that the evening darkens, with a keen wind.

II   THE LITTLE DARLING[*]

When I found you in the chill twilight a vandal
had splodged red paint on your breast—or was it
someone had thought your heart bled? You began
as a clay street-arab moulded for a fête
and cast in plaster for temporary exhibition,
but remained in more lasting bronze because people
liked you (then)—and fittingly you became
the focus for sixties' meetings of rebellious "provos"
who hoped for freedom (and houses). But in a café
on Leidseplein a Dutchman, enthusiastic
about the Historical Museum and primed
with facts about the Begijnhof did not remember
that you existed. And so by accident
I saw you lonely when looking for a bookshop.

There are no Beguines left to care now—though the ambiance
is tended by almswomen and well-behaved students—
but their candle-lit chapel, once secret, is now open
while the neatly Protestant Church that disinherited
their devotion seems locked except for concerts.

Before that once furtive altar I shall light you a candle,
asking the Virgin's help—since this place is discreet—
though the Magdalene might understand better.

Under those towered, closed churches and fat burgher buildings
is only sand in water, like the bone and blood
that kindled your smile: the trees root in the mud

---

*   '*t Lieverdje*, statue by Carol Kneulman in Spui, Amsterdam

and the plinth for your limbs is embedded in it, so that your spirit,
as in Van Gogh's poor labourers and Vermeer's homely servants
can sing in the distant carillon (to *Greensleeves*)
"Alas, my love, you do me wrong, to cast
me off discourteously," I will mend that wrong,
keeping alight your taper in the heart's apse.

III   THE CITY[*]

The sea is level, surly:
it threatens turbulence
that the clouds realise,
vast in waves of grey
convoluted black.

What immortal hand
dare divide
one from the other?

Yet this line of light
with white dome, gold column,
out of the underground
crystallises
genesis.

The work of mind
emboldened
human fingers
to make from this maw
a womb:

frail beings
impregnated
that amorphous darkness.

Pray for them now and at the hour of
their living.

---

*   Painting by August Strindberg exhibited in the Rijksmuseum Vincent Van Gogh,
Amsterdam, April 1987

IV   GIDEON AND REBECCA[*]

Unkempt, fair-haired, she chubby, he a bit squat:
her skimpy blue anorak reveals a red cardigan
but its matching jeans have faded; he wears black and grey.
Wiser than we think, younger than they pretend,
they stand on filthy stones, making their own world.
Leaning cross-legged on a graffiti'd wall, she watches—
arms outspread, open-handed, as though inviting.
He has his leathered back to the camera
and his unseen hands seem occupied in what
we cannot be sure about and doesn't matter—
what is important is innocent rapport.

Ages ago Isaac and Rebekah
met after journeyings and family treaties—
the drawing of water for camels, the offering
of a ring weighing half a shekel and two bracelets:
fortunately when they met they loved
and Isaac was comforted for his mother's death.

An earlier Gideon knew what a river told.

Rebecca asks no earnest from Gideon
and they do without camels, but their togetherness
is though experimental and rather relaxed
as trusting as in former epochs. No jewels or cattle,
but the same reciprocity well

where pebbles generate rings in accepting depths.

---

*   Photograph by Jack Jacobs, 1971, published by Art Unlimited, Amsterdam.

100

V   PHOTOGRAPH TAKEN ON A COACH TOUR
     FROM AMSTERDAM

You can snap the four windmills only from the bridge
where the coach cannot stop, though eternity might grace
their posture, sails and purpose. The red ridge
of an adjoining house makes each a whole place
but jointly with the blue-grey river they form an edge
to an achieved land defending togetherness,
the creation of solidarity from loose mud
and sand that could trickle. It's like a recumbent nude
that differs from constituent bone, flesh and blood
by being an identity, so that what is made
matters more than the medium—which could be paint
and in reality the girl not be there at all
except as a concept which will not respond:
pictured birds cannot fly but those sails moved—
it is only when photographed that they seem still
and not fulfilling their aim. We made a rhyme
of what was fluid and temporary as water
in the river, whose permanence is never the same.
Eternity is not a moment in time
in the sense of an instant, but a force that moves,
rotating mud, blood, skin, water and flesh in a breath
that behoves to be but not now or for always is:
the rhyme is internal, not fixing the line's end.
It is only for the dying that time stops, and their death
is like one train passing another but at no time level.
The crocus and snowdrop stir in the same wind
(that we do not see) but wave in different air.
The ripple in the cornfield moves through but is not the wheat.

All this seems a long way from windmills but is not:
An English mill grinds corn but Dutch ones are often pumps.
A dyke is a bank or the hollow made by digging one
and becomes a ditch, but serving as boundary
in Yorkshire is a wall, and can be a band

of intrusive rock, a basalt sill called whin—
which elsewhere is the gorse growing near it. A sill
is also where the lock-gates stop, managing water.
A language bends to the landscape it copes with— it is
how the mind fixes a dream, like the chemicals
that stabilise these four windmills and make this picture
to remind the eyes of what they once glimpsed,
the spirit of what it once felt—deep in the being
the perpetual rhyming of events achieves
the strata of an existence, above which
is all that alluvium, which is what is seen
and thought the only reality—but here
the consolidation of alluvium makes real
what was a dream before. One should not allow
images their unfettered fancy without pumps,
dykes, watercourses, high and low level drains
and the paraphernalia of logic—Pygmalion
could not couple with stone and only in legend
did Aphrodite rescue him from those nymphets
who deluded nympholepts by posing as warm statues.

The point this landscape makes, if you understand it,
is that whatever dreams or philosophies
it may inspire, men should always keep a firm grip
on what is—or they find it is not there.
Home is an idea but we have to build it
and keep the weather out. The eternal may be
safe in itself, but its being in time is for us
to ensure: we are on a bridge from polder to polder.

Forms are not there to blight
ideas by preening wit:

Pantoums are not
what you have thought.
The form you fight
will open out.

What you have thought
and dearly bought
will open out
like flowers to light;

and dearly bought
the poem will shoot
like flowers to light
earth's sepia night.

The poem will shoot
since thought will root:
earth's sepia night
feeds form to fruit

Pantoum and villanelle
weave art to quell
what makes the human state
disintegrate.

103

VI   FINALE

What for no second is may yet be true:
here on flat sand men raised the tower and spire
to mingle with empty sky they saw as blue
with angelic cloud—mere droplets in cold air.

From fluids coursing in flesh they hallowed love.
Words carved a form for things to be themselves.
Elsewhere haphazard rocks achieved a cove:
here men firm quays where loose mud slips and shelves.

Into a world of granite, slate and shale,
roach, swallows, sunflowers and the nutrient corn
like pink-edged shell or self-sown harebell, frail
as a baby's skull, the human mind is born,

which, unlocated, with its body builds
from random molecules swirling in space
the appearance of solidarity, and gilds
pinnacles heralding home as created place.

IKEN CLIFF*

Botwulf, patron of wayfarers,
founder here by Ica's hill
of a monastery later infernalised
by Viking raiders, I find peace
in the meanderings of tidal streams,
the ventriloquy of oystercatchers,
and the tumbling or statuesque waiting
of lapwings, whose desolations
are as widespread as the sixty-four churches
praising God in your name—including
your stump of stone at Boston.
Like a tern you wandered, paused, dived
and out of the anonymous sea
retrieved faith silver like little fishes.

I speak now because I need you:
you are in history with no biography.

Your teaching influenced three royal virgins—
who might have been happier paddling
for painters of Books of pagan Hours
who like Wilson Steer professionalised
their wistfulness on sands at Walberswick,
or lying under the druidic oaks
that also hallow this primeval hoe
as Carmina of contradictory record—
but inspired Liobsynde, abbess of Wenlock,
who passed your torch to holy Ceolfrith
who at Wearmouth lit it for Bede.
Yet of your life we know nothing except

---

*   654 In this year king Anna was killed; Botwulf began to build a monastery at
Icanhoh. — *Anglo-Saxon Chronicle* (Parker)

your hallowing many stones before dying,
though your head, recovered by Ulfkitel
at the king's command, was enshrined at Ely
and other portions at St. Edmundsbury, Westminster,
and with all of your brother Adulf at Thorney.

Somehow this dismembering is appropriate:
you wandered, founded, spread faith, and were scattered.

Like Aidan, Cuthbert, Chad you denied maidens
the joy of their bodies but preserved love
as a stronghold for the lives of men and women
who knew otherwise. You were a candle
in a great darkness, a beacon light
to guide over treacherous sea among marshes
attractive to such as me, but pathless.

I speak now because I need you:
patron of wayfarers, here at Iken,
at Boston, and in the London of Christopher Wren,
you are an influence but an anonymity,
thus patron also of teachers, poets, vagabonds
who rescue others in city streets or beside
lanes in the rural loneliness of twilight,

So are we all wayfarers, all pilgrims;
so are we all dismembered, scattered;
so do our echoes bring comfort, peace,
hope to light torches of love after
we are dust or have become reeds
for the wind to rustle, as beside this river
which turns, winds, aims falsely but
reaches eventually after the formless mud
the hard red shingle and the open sea—

106

and is also a channel bringing barges
past mourning Slaughden which the sea ravaged
and this port, now two locked
sheds and the rotting relics of a pier,
home safe to the bridge where reed-buntings
twitter beside the graciousness of Snape.

History is made of dismembered relics
of the biography of what was alive,
like Botwulf, Wilson Steer, or the women
riding their horses into waves by Shingle Street
or girls and boys on beaches in the July sun.

FISHERMEN'S MEMORIAL, GLOUP, YELL, SHETLAND

We stand by the widow's stone statue, acknowledging
that in life we seek safe harbours: looking down
on this sheltered fiord one would think some god had made it—
as a haven or as a reminder of faith misplaced?

She stands, holding her nursling, peering seaward
as possibly did many, years ago,
when fifty-eight men in boats from Haroldswick
and other places sought refuge here from a hurricane
and were drowned in wreck. Some postcards
show the statue in sunlight, but better
are those which, from behind here, gaze into mist
and hills that might be storm or clouds like hills.
Why do we lament what happened in 1881
as though it were yesterday? It is not a symbol—
it is something more: we should feel the same
at that memorial near Rhosllanercrugog
of the Gresford colliery disaster and in other places
where women and children lost the men who loved
and the men lost the life they were giving. One asks
why did they live at all if only to die
in the gaining of a livelihood? And politicians
talk with interminable glibness of growth and profit
as though their reality were not what all the time
bases love's hope on the flux or strata of death.

An interrupting voice insists that death
comes anyway; all that oppression or poverty causes
is an earlier or different incidence; as Beckett saw,
women give birth astride a grave, and elegy
for golden groves or passing beauties is grief
for Margaret who sees them unleaving or fading:
that loveliness, life, love are threatened and evanescent
is a commonplace, just as is the realisation
that human beings live by struggle, often by competition.

108

Disasters happen and it may dangerous to distort them
or twist the fact of the ruthlessness of struggling men
into propaganda for political controversy. In both
the catastrophic and the pitiless there seems cause to cry out
in prayer to a possibly indifferent heaven or a god
who would delude the suffering into nobility or bring as salvation
remedy in some eternal dream or a sustaining promise
of later but elusive redress, an unsure road through time.
John Cowper Powys proclaimed that the astronomical world
is not all there is, but can man or woman
really live in the non-earthly, non-astronomical
except on an earthly basis? Man may not live
by bread alone but dies alone without bread.
The unastronomical gospel could be one of fellow-suffering,
god's son as companion slave, to sustain a value
more beautiful than the oppressor's but unavailing:
it triumphs in eternity but not in history,
to enthrall a spirit in an animal dying by the clock.

We have seen that political movements to thwart men's evil
can be undone by man's evil since they are movements of men.
Hence Ozymandias may be joined in the desert
by monuments to dictators for the human good, both sneering
because the effort to be monumental is a process
of becoming both cruel and hollow, and the Pyramids,
Canary Wharf and all technological grandeur
are based, as Mumford saw, on the exaltation
of a machine over men; such cannot be a cure
for the suffering or weak loneliness of the human
in a world of alien power. What is needed
is not faith in history or the glory of man's achievement
nor enslavement by law of science, evolution or economics
but their contradiction by love, by a recognition
of what Peter Kropotkin discovered as mutual aid,
affection that is fellow-feeling written into the biological.

We were told that houses should be built not on sand but on rock,
but man's fate is what happens when the rocks move
or, as here, when the storm overwhelms the haven.
The bases have earthquakes, devout beliefs
may lead to threats or murder, since misunderstanding
clouds charity and brilliant thought confuses.

May whatever stirs people to create memorials
to lament the dead or to sacrifice for the living
as in widespread charities, cause also the human prayer,
the leaning on one another, the recognition
of who we are where we are in a world that has more
than at first appears or deluded masters taught us.

Let us go down to the shore in the recognition
that the sea will not say anything, that the fiord
was the work of geology and time, not of God's providence,
and growing a crop on the fields is the work of man
with seeds that evolved but whose use was realised
as people now all over the world in varied
but agonised societies could realise the grains of hope
in support of each other in spite of clouds that threaten
storms over protective headlands or breakers dashing against rocks.
We can stand against the gale, looking out with vision
as well as anxiety, like the widow cradling her nursling.
Her prayer is also ours but we can channel the solidarity
and the universality of grief that enables people to set
her here as a memorial into what may deliver
mankind from itself in realising that deep fellowship
among all who face tempest lights breakwaters that hallow peace.

V

CONVERSATIONAL ELEGIES
FOR A
TYNESIDE KID

CONVERSATIONAL ELEGIES FOR A TYNESIDE KID
— EPIGRAPHS AND A NOTE

I

Experiencing and judging are as distinct as breathing and biting. To judge men by whether they accept history or are ashamed of it. People can only redeem *one another.* That is why God takes a human disguise.

from ELIAS CANETTI — *THE HUMAN PROVINCE*
(André Deutsch, 1985; trans. © Seabury Press Inc.)

It didn't occur to me to bow down before the performing horses of history.

Georg Büchner to his fiancée
(Quoted by Idris Parry in *ANIMALS OF SILENCE*
Oxford University Press, 1972)

II

CHILD POVERTY UP

As many as 30 % of children in Britain are living below the poverty line, according to statistics just released by the Department of Health and Social Security, writes Robert Taylor. The number has risen dramatically since 1979, from 2,370,000 to 3,880,000—a jump of 64%. Up to 400,000 children now live in households existing below the Supplementary Benefit level (£68.00 a week for a two-child family, after rent). Since the DHSS statistics were drawn up, the position is believed to have become even worse.

THE OBSERVER, Sunday 2nd November, 1986.

RAT GNAWS GIRL

A girl was in hospital yesterday after being bitten four times by a rat while she lay sleeping at her home in Ryknield Way, South Shields, Tyne and Wear. One of six-year-old Emma Cutter's toes had been bitten through to the bone.

THE GUARDIAN, News-in-Brief, Saturday 30th September, 1989

III

The true enemy of man is generalisation.
The true enemy of man, so-called History,
Attracts and terrifies with its plural number.
Don't believe it. Cunning and treacherous,
History is not, as Marx told us, anti-nature,
And if a goddess, a goddess of blind fate.
The little skeleton of Miss Jadwiga, the spot
Where her heart was pulsating. This only
I set against necessity, law, theory.

> CZESLAW MILOSZ—Lecture IV of 'Six Lectures in Verse' in
> THE COLLECTED POEMS (1931-1987) (Penguin Books, 1988)

IV

Et qu'importent les maux et les heures démentes,
Et les cuves de vice où la cité fermente,
Si quelque jour, du fond des brouillards et des voiles,
Surgit un nouveau Christ, en lumière sculpté,
Qui soulève vers lui l'Humanité
Et la baptise au feu de nouvelles étoiles.

> EMIL VERHAEREN—end of 'L'Ame de la Ville' in
> LES VILLES TENTACULAIRES (1895)

What matter the wrongs and the demented hours
Or the vats of vice where the city ferments
If one day, out of thick depths of fog and smoke
Rises a new Christ, sculpted in light,
Who lifting humanity towards himself
Baptises it in the fire of new stars.

(Trans. BMH.)

V

The extract from Sir William Petty quoted in 'Elegy IV' is taken from
HUMPHREY JENNINGS — PANDAEMONIUM (The Coming of the Machine
as Seen by Contemporary Observers) edited by Mary-Lou Jennings and
Charles Madge and published in 1985 by André Deutsch. There is a later
edition in Picador.

114

ELEGY I

You disappeared behind a door almost opposite
Shieldfield's forbidding reliable chapel and hall
where dances, forbidden like gambling on Methodist premises,
happened full-bloodedly as "rhythmic exercises"
that briefly put colour into six-to-a-slum-room lives.
I had caused a brief disturbance—suddenly dashing
out of a respectable group through the gaudy, sweaty
gaggle of those not usually seen at worship
to where, though about fourteen, an ember with obscured fire,
you waited for a wind to strip the ash. For some
it was as though we'd taken your scanty, yellow
clothes off then and there on the Sunday School floor.
When the quick waltz ended it was cream-bun time—
I got a plate but you'd left. The door shut
as I threw the plate in the gutter. It's no use now
to go back—the goodsyard that kids watched, risking
the precipitous boundary wall, was bombed, Gehinnom
transmuted decades ago; and, besides, the worthies
called you an alley kitten: like the lithe
charming self-disentanglers that inspirited
that city you'll have gone under or come through,
since you flashed dark eyes and like me by then
were probably a bit smelly—might be now
though differently.
                              Why do I remember
so vividly that I can walk those streets
without shutting my eyes, any time, and see
the barefoot children, the women both heavy and gaunt
and the rare work-haunted men, who seemed to hide
or had gone elsewhere; they did not sit on The Green
like Old John with white hair, though it echoed at times
with innocence attaining experience. Employed memories
do not help the unemployed: *nessun maggior dolore*
than knowing one threw away stale bread.
                              And what
does memory achieve for me when it doesn't

115

merely create the neurosis of not being the boy
I was, to do what I now know, as another,
was what I ought to have done when someone else?
There is no limit to this, it is dangerous: yet something
urges to seek what will come of it. What water
from Round Hill and Cross Fell reaches the Tyne Bridge?
What Pennine and Cheviot snows wash the quayside, drift with refuse,
sewage and sawdust from Kielder to anonymous sea?

I sometimes think of people who are imprisoned
for murder, rape, or subtle fraud committed
many years before they're found out. In a way
they are not guilty: the water round the Hexham salmon
is not the flow from a Nentsberry leadmine.
It's as though the monk, Thomas Merton, writing a letter
to Ernesto Cardenal ("one of the most significant
voices of the two Americas") were abruptly extradited
because the Cambridge shopgirl who'd borne his son
was proved to be under age when she conceived.

But the ripening of wisdom, achievement of balance,
some "little, nameless, unremembered acts
of kindness and of love" may have become possible
because the proceeds of fraud paid for education
or enabled that country cottage where God spoke;
the early sexual experience possibly facilitated
harmony in a family. Must hard labour expiate
or pretend to deter others when it cannot
save the defrauded from poverty, or rescue
the mother and child from a bomb that had nothing
to do with a Trappist monk or her being fifteen?
One cannot alter the river, flow it back, but
to argue from this is dangerous—you were fourteen,
I sixteen—so possibly something justifies
somehow trying to preserve laws, though the action

116

of benevolent human design is like caging
robins because there are kestrels. Beating bars kills.
Shall the universe be stopped because of a trapped mole,
the Idwal Slabs be unpraised or even levelled because
my friend fell? I remember a despairing boy
proud of having crawled underground from one ventilation
hole, along, past the shaft to the leadmine, to another
(twenty yards further on) saying it would not matter
if he'd fallen through. It would have done to me
though now I do not care to know where he is:
the water reflects the harbour lights, is not
cold in the gloom of that gallery.

I used to think that the wise should arrange life
like a vast boarding-school—but now Illich
shows that the world is a vast schoolroom, different
because the senior teachers are ignorant. Possibly
it would still be tyranny if the head were Lao-Tzu.
A pupil once asked me what Blake would have done
in a situation that threatened ideas we shared;
I replied that Blake would not have run a school—
though someone has to. But let it not be for long
lest the starling's wing tarnish. Berdyaev would tell
how freedom, the natural habitat of the spirit,
may be dangerous: servitude comforts the timid
who unlike robins will not flutter at the bars.

You would love, then, an aviary of pacified canaries?
Rather 1930's Shieldfield than compulsory Heaven.
To the Nent again:
                    the London Lead Company,
a Quaker firm, made Nenthead a model village,
the social club replacing the village alehouse,
and all went well with the pattern until
they sold out to La Vielle Montagne Zinc,

In a few years Nenthead's illegitimacy rate
was the highest in England—and when I knew it
various inhabitants didn't bother to marry
and I wondered if the beautiful dark kitchenmaid
had an incestuous grandfather—happiness dwindled,
some dust obscured her patterned inner burning.

The whole valley could be cut off from Alston by snow
as Alston from England except for the railway.
But the men scraped crow-coal from little tumuli
while their wives ran "the farm"; a community lived
as valuable a life as those who plan
New York to Tokyo through space in two hours
when no one can reach a sick woman near Buxton
because of ice. I believe in original sin
reluctantly, unconvinced by legendary theology
but simply because mankind's false priorities
provide the basis of a civilisation as doomed
as ever were those that left their picturesque ruins
to pad our culture: the Heights of Macchu Picchu
may be replaced by the Sidney Opera House
or piles of brick in Toxteth—Moctezuma,
the Incas, Thatcher, Pizarro, the Chinese War-Lords,
Reagan and Gorbachov remembered as symbols
(Mexican in intricacy) of advancing catastrophe.
Yet a child is born in Ethiopia, Cuba,
Iceland or Bangladesh who might lead them,
unless she became an alcoholic whore
to die when firebombs lit a Shieldfield alley.
We are back there again!
                       There are two concepts—
the Earth and the World—Shieldfield is the World,
what man has made of and on the Earth,
which for me is the sphagnum moss on Nent fells,
the marshes of Lindsey, Bodmin Moor, the *bryniau*

and *nentydd* around Aber, Ogwen, Brecon—
though these are symbols, like Clent, a Worcestershire hill
on the summit of which the Earl of Lyttleton
constructed "druidic" remains because, as the Cornish
dialect has it, they belong to be there
as prayers to the Earth to speak—against the World
or to enable the proper World that the Earth
and people on the earth would wish to have,
a world where their and the Earth's voice are heard
not drowned in the aimless purposefulness of machines,
for which, that wealth might accrue, the skilled masters,
ship's carpenters, welders, professionals of Shieldfield,
starved hidden in idleness when I played games
with their anaemic children—as they do now
when snow on this Nidderdale bog reminds me of struggling
through Jesmond ice or by Blagill walled with drifts.
With the power cut off and Social Security Snoopers
prowling to catch a man in the room, your daughter
may draw the curtains as I pull down the blinds
not knowing what earth intends or the World is for.

As I pause at the twilit window I see that the snow
has embossed a perfect wheel on the lichened end
of a rectangular trough for prolific stonecrop;
it asks the how and the why we ask of all—
adventurously (like *sedum acre*) when young,
with quizzing "maturity" in our middle age,
when old half-musing, half-despairingly.

The relentless snow puts a clockface between friends—
the flakes like minutes and hours disappear in the air,
their dead accumulation muffles the ground,
marks then obscures the footfall, blows, freezes, melts
like the years between this starshine and that grey sunlight
both stirring unconsuming fire in icicles

119

here on these eaves or there on the rusting chains
of swings that even in Winter tempted limbs
to exult through the chapping airs on Shieldfield Green.

But in upland winter sunsets the waterfalls
between Nenthead and Nentsberry seemed to burn
to mock the flow in pillars of static light.

ELEGY II

I want to keep your image not in my mind
but in me, even beyond that point of danger;
somehow it is necessary so that I avoid
philosophies that synthesise you away
psychologies that explain but leave you out
there in the north-east wind, while your yellow dress
clinging snow-wet sharpens the cauld blast.
It belonged in the dance which was a ritual
frenzy of maenad and satyr re-possessing,
like fauns and Pan who maddens those lost in woods,
creatures of the earth astray on the boarded floor,
the pavement or the tarmac where bubbles revealed
the unextinguished thistle, dandelion or goat's beard
which though despised, seek and echo the sun.
You obsess as a basement daffodil, too soon,
your stalk too ready to fracture, twirling, inviting—
though someone may have plucked and made you a lady
at ease with cars and videos in Gosforth;
there are two worlds in which I wander alien—
your first I do not escape: there hides the meaning.

Memory mixes the seasons because it tries
to make a pattern in paragraphs, like the theories
I am resisting. I wanted you in me
and me in you, although this would have been
to summon the nasturtium to bloom in grim December
after the blackening frosts. Hence I persist
in seeking the fact rather than the explanation.
Plotinus, greatest of interpreters by metaphor,
said "Be sure that your theory of God
does not lessen him," Let me always remember:

> a greenfinch, dead in the yard after the gale,
> rigid, bright-feathered, like a leaf,
> to be swept with the leaves.

A lone being
that felt
flashed green-golden,
will not again flash
or feel.

Why lament?
Birds in Winter
without much suffering (we are told)
starve, just stop.
This is the nature of things.

Gales cleanse: Winter is rhythmic fallow,
sleep of seed.
Darkness by contrast
enables light;
death is life's needed shadow.

Tell that to the greenfinch.

I did not take the trouble to discover—
without upsetting the world I could not discover—
whether you froze in the basement, or if the rats
nibbled you dying and gnawed your feet before
you were found, like the child of the woman who showed me
her room in the house where Charles II stayed
while golfing on the Shield Field. There was a door
blocking the tunnel believed to go to a castle—
there the rats bred, and awaited food in darkness.
Your lips, your thighs, your feet, your yellow frock
were fixed in a pattern historians diagnose
as the Thirties, in which our dancing had no meaning.
A Minister's son, romantic, instinctive, and a budding
scamp must seem like the repetitive wallpaper

of a room of state where, like the tunnel rats,
the important wait or act or re-enact.

    A frog lying squashed among the battering sticks
    (near Hohegeiss—
    Sorge east of the border, Zorge on the west)
    and a butterfly dead on the path.
    Grey men draw separating lines
    straight or sweeping mathematically.
    Frog hopped, tortoiseshell flew
    zigzag, being
    alive

Those who try to cross borders tread on landmines.

Too real city! Poets make cities unreal
to escape from nightmare into middle distance
or to mould their painful vision into art
expressing agony in ironic image.
Even in dreadful night there are little lamps,
petty "empires of light" that tempt revival
of the justification of spirit which was dumb
and prevent abandon of self, of every street,
of every living person in dark water
suddenly become a threat or a salvation.
Like sleep, like death this comes, the eyelids close
inside being: another automaton talks, stalks
over neon pavements , not looking up
at the river of stars bedding the timeworn gorge
of rocky houses. Only the rain
can make the stone reflect, the wakened skin
remind the flesh ...

City of bridges, which, on the dangerous quay
or through the filth of Byker we walked *beneath:*

other people walked on bridges
to reach roads leading
to further bridges.
In this hole we lived
on river's edge, under,
where the arch
grounds.

Bridges conjugate
future tenses,
holes present and conditional.
"Should water rise, I drown."

But we saw their roads,
where they went,
looking up learned how
bridges are made,
fathomed why, in the way
those who use them
cannot know.

Many kids had calyciform frocks or loved those who had
and cuddled under spans of traffic or behind
St. Mary's ruined chapel, unsepalling before
they fuelled or were crushed by the wheels, welded or sailed
the achieved, evanescent ships (while I retreated
into sonnets of imaginative truth).
                                        What is dangerous
is nostalgia ignoring the river: one should recall
where one was and with whom and where one went,
who one was, who they were and what awaited.
It is all very well to say that experience
is an arch wherethrough gleams an untravelled world,
but some made the bricks and went on pointing the arch—
not all are kings to grace the Happy Isles.

Each moment one person is—and then is not:
you are not what you were; for what we were
I'll go back to the stanchions that I wrote about
a few years after the dancing ended—between
those Hérédian sonnets the prologue to the play:

> We are the pillars that support the world,
> the Atlas on whom rest the cities of men,
> and all their hopes and fears and country pleasures
> their wars their peace their marriages and divorces
> work themselves out upon the little stage
> that we support. They do not understand.
> They do not know us, for we are the pillars.
> None know the pillars that uphold the world.
> When the pillars have cried Caesar hath wept
> and shortly levied taxes for wars in Gaul.
> The pillars ye have always with you, and thus
> you know they can be neglected while in Wales,
> or when the harvest is good and men build new barns
> which increase the weight of the world upon the pillars.
> We the pillars do not occur in the play—
> we merely support the stage and do not matter;
> we are neither heroic characters nor villainous;
> we merely remain, and will remain, until
> the weight becomes too great for us to bear.

Typical Thirties, of course, but it meant what it said
and since critics sneer the wheels of suffering turn
to where they were and therefore my mind seeks the river,
treads to the source, mid-valley, or swirl by the quay.

It is all very well to poeticise about calyxes
and sentimental unsepalling, all very well
for that matter to regard working men as pillars—
I take nothing back—but one river,

125

the branching artery of Shieldfield and Byker,
flows in the bodies of women and in their spirit—
the first not imagined as flowers but known as muscles
and the other not a question of eternal souls
but remarkable for an indomitable persistence
that creates, rescues, preserves, whose primary quality
is being always here or there when wanted.

I read of a woman who bore twenty-two children,
and had a lodger, the husband being rarely there
but off with someone probably fresher, or in the pub
since the family lived in one room—and at times
one child would wait in a coffin to be collected
while another was being born. After each event
she would get on with the cleaning or cook a meal,
helped briefly by a neighbour, because no matter
what one family unreasonably demanded there was always time
to help next door in a crisis. In a time of snow
the pavement would be swept; before the dance
the daffodil frock would be washed and the cub's uniform
ready for tomorrow; between the drying and airing
what food could be had for what money there was
would be made somehow attractive with a labour
unrivalled in the kitchens of Hilton Hotels.
And a kid going out would be given a halfpenny.

Unsepalling may mature seed, but it is as though
from a sucker or cutting that grows each original tree
unique though forming copses, individuals
yet seeming a species. Each has her own gnarled,
possibly wry boughs, like a broom-tree I saw
once at the edge of an ancient garden, twisted,
dry and about to die, but on green twigs,
rare but achieved unbroken, it flowered red.

126

Even young, and not yet hard-faced but soft-hearted,
women would oblige the lonely, the friends of brothers,
or those nearer, and continue through the battering years
whose months are days made of hours and minutes
occupied by the necessity to enable
the continuity of living. The world
may become a waste-tip burdening the earth, but through it
run, unfailing, veins in which gold would be pollution.
Among the pallid or blackened ash gleam sapphires
with clean-cut faces which flash blue and which no rat
or government official can pulverise, gnaw or dissolve.

Flow, river, bearing the lighted ships past shadowy allotments
where among necessary potatoes could bloom, deserved, the rose.

ELEGY III

At Christmas in the brutal war I stayed three nights
with a kindly parson and his welcoming wife
in one of those pastoral villages of Northumberland
that face away from the granite Cheviots
and open their roads like arms to the dawn from the sea.
As befitted profession and place he was shepherd to people,
caring for villagers and soldiers in an army camp.
He had spent earlier probationary years
with my pacifist father and like-minded colleagues
and now took pride and care in pointing out
that he had no extreme views and admired
the decently-living recruits, who kept off the beer
and were therefore worthy. After respectable
well-regulated days I set off in a bus,
with doors frozen open, to the bombed city
on the way to children who had found refuge
from fire and explosion amid Nent's treacherous snows.
In a café a young, widowed, half-German waitress
brought me coffee, food , whiskey while I showed her
photographs bought in Wooler of the quietly deep
water of the threatening Till, and of the peat-stained, stony
fell-shadowed rills and haggs of Skirl Naked Valley
(my host's good picnic-place for a dry Summer).

I have spent fifty years failing to resolve this.

My city childhood surprises friends, who remark
that I seem alien to that nativity—
for I was twice born, though not in a Hindu sense:
After I'd survived zeppelins in my first year
I was taken to Easington Colliery, Thorne, Belper—
and there I was a little child, beginning
to emerge conscious in Worksop shortly
before my second birth in what I thought
was to be my own place. One dies and is reborn
many times, unless one is moribund from the start

(world conditioned) but certain births establish
what being rises in minor resurrections.

Worksop saw a stirring within a womb (lined with
adoring girls) but the naked child emerged
into the Jesmond snow: in Heaton and Shieldfield
that womb had ceased to shelter. Thus I belong
irreversibly to that second nativity
which was not in my own place, for I had moved
almost ceaselessly from town to town and was alien
to each and therefore to my own beginning.

"Nothing, like something, happens anywhere"
to those who do not dig deep, or forget (protesting
against others' boasting) what nothings happened.
The nothings form equations one cannot analyse
into pure integral elements, never mind solve.

The children, calyciform or ugly, went to school
and living education such as too few now long for
could grace the despised Thirties, though it reached
not very many. The chariots of desire
at least were not anathema. Heaton Secondary School
more than contemporary institutions for training,
illuminated, led out, brought forth, cultivated,
instructed but encouraged to flower: and I set down names
that they may be at least once recorded, and in the annals
of a burnt century I hope these charred pages
will survive in some museum as a memorial,
unlike "intolerably nameless names" and some names
which, though better forgotten, became History—
that record of people whose acts obscure what matters.

Headmasters exaggerate themselves: their importance
is less than they think, since most of what occurs

in a sane school is an unforecast interaction
of who and what happens to be there—that is how
schooldays are life preparing for life, with someone
to effect a few barriers and necessary repairs.
(I knew a good headmaster who when he inspected
the boys' lavatories seemed to wear heavy boots.
Another had a notice on his usually half-open
study door that wisely read, "Don't tell me".)
F. R. Barnes regulated but without
seeming to do so, generated an ambiance.
"Peace Studies" had not been invented, but took place
(just as psychology is to be found in Shakespeare)
in that pupils saw themselves part of the world,
working in it, not victims or adjuncts. They probably forgot
when brutality took over. But two people
have that immortality that lives in others
being transmitted.
                    Israel Simpson revealed
French clarity, order, purpose as a second medium
for emotion and thought: none need be restricted
to one manner of saying. Romain Rolland,
Lamartine, Vigny, Hugo, Leconte de Lisle
became paths in the mind, Verlaine an overgrown park.
And he criticised my declamation of Isaiah
in morning assembly—a passage he had chosen—
as I had missed the pathos, the human cry
for Jahweh to split the heavens and come down,
not hide his face from men in clouds of glory.
One cannot make such things as evocative
as backstreet scamps, but the simple prose
is that seeing things in focus is poetic
in that the obsessively incarnate begins to create.
Tagore tells a story of a saint who has reached
the peak of blessedness after years of struggle
but wishes to leave the aridity of transcendence

for the girl who gathered twigs and brought him fruit
which had shrivelled outside his austere hermitage.
Ernest Dyer brought drama into the mind
and the mind into drama: we lived, with Karel Capek,
the necessary coming of love among machines,
the truth, the hope. We learned that the mind is human
"Which seeks a 'soul of goodness' in things ill
Or in himself or others"—for Shelley stirred
always within that golden head, as now
in me—and in others. I recall writing,
at Nent Hall among fells such as he loved,
when he later died (of exposure in a hospital
while waiting for strained muscles to be examined):

> "Soon will the clod that beauty of body cover
> and high thoughts seem to be less than the trees' stride
> over the grave's hummock or the broken coping
> of a forgotten house. Alone we die,
> leaving our lives living in others' hoping ..."

Some time afterwards I happened to see
near an ordinary road two blossoming hawthorns
growing out of an oak—the seeds had fallen
where birds perched by a riven branch. Red May
seemed to flower out of White May, since both
were rooted in that ancient tree, itself
gathering the compost of a thousand years.
What sap would feed a berry of mistletoe
that lighted there? My Bible Christian forebears
(who, surprised at the year-end surplus of six-and-eightpence,
resolved to evangelise South Wales—and did it)
were as alien to Shelley as oak to hawthorn is,
and Rabindranath Tagore (whose Wardour Street English
infused an unascetic religion) would have seemed to Shelley
a fungus on sad superstition, My words, my acts

are leaves or seeds of a remarkable tree,
natural but denying that classification
which fixes the world as unchanging, unredeemed,
and not redeemable: the irresponsible flight
of birds knows better, as does the wind that brought
to bombsites Elizabethan willowherb.

By the time I was in my own place I was moved
into a world of dustbin factories, near
to Shenstone's Wassell Grove, which, like my births
and the people within my mind, seemed far away.
But within me martins planed in a secret wind
over streets where disconsolate children found no twigs.

Dark-eyed girl behind a slammed door, what was it?
Merely to put me into you, like a dog with a bitch
on Shieldfield Green? That is the easiest answer,
the technical answer, psycho-analytic,
physiological—the rest is décor.

I knew a South African research scientist
who worked for ten-minute stretches in the Bodleian
then had coffee and a cigarette. Considering
my friend's confession that his hoped-for adultery
was hardly satisfactory he remarked
that the aim was ejaculation of sperm
into a woman— and this had taken place,
so success was satisfactory. I wondered
why he could only contemplate such matters
in bursts of brief duration: technically,
he said, it illustrated the fact
that the human mind can only concentrate
for ten minutes. Well, I suppose that is
time enough for a somewhat mechanical
escape from sexual pressure, time enough

for a computer thought: the rest is décor,
Victorian or modern elegance of the loo.

Day dreaming down darkening streets even a boy
soliloquises imagined conversations
showing the search is for meaningful revelation,
the unveiling of inner being, not merely
for uninhibited touching: I seemed to talk
to someone recognised but also unknown
till the reply was the rattle of a cornering tram
or the coming of a train through the deep cutting
on the other side of the road, its brief stop
by the hidden platform and its chattering through the distance
to a silence that was for me its destination.

That image again—the red may flowers for the lonely,
as for me a twilit bush near Jesmond Dene Road.
I had wandered to a turning and found another road
which crossed a third to slope down to the river,
but half-way there a plain-clothes detective
with a light brown macintosh and a disguising pipe
crossed the road to take my reluctant arm
and say, "This is no place for a kid like you.
Where are you going?" "I'm not going anywhere—
I'm just walking." "Then try walking back."
So I went miles back and found the red hawthorn.

But in school good friends prevented exploration
becoming solipsist reduction: the casual
interchange of thought made intellect thrive,
the self live by forgetting self—the white may bloomed.
Let petals from both blow alien to Shieldfield
where basement daffodils don't hear Hérédian sonnets
(how could they, guarding ovules awaiting anthers
before heavy feet tread, the dust chokes,

or ice cracks the yellowed stem?). The detached blossom
drifts with the eddying wind in stony gutters.

What was it that made Katharine Bruce Glasier
at whose feet (literally) I sat, reading
these emotions wrapped in rhythms from Francis Thompson,
thoughts from Shelley and colour from Verlaine,
perceive the intricate taproots of these hawthorns?
A comet from known but distant constellations,
she rekindled this galaxy—while washing up
in a flaking stone sink—I was too enthralled
to remember one used a bowl. (The others
had had to meet in a socialist committee.)

"Adolescent" is how T. S. Eliot describes
those lines of Shelley echoing Dante and Plato,
"I never was attached to that great sect
Whose doctrine is, that each man should select
Out of the crowd a mistress or a friend,
And all the rest, though fair and wise, commend
To cold oblivion,"—and his subsequent words
prove that he did not read the text in order.
Hating his love of Shelley, which must have disturbed
his careful construct of something on which to rejoice
out of a life as *bête* as Shelley's, he reacted
against prosaic lines in a flawed poem in which
a man obsessed by veiled nakedness confused
sex, Platonism, political freedom and a search
for spiritual solidarity amid mutinous flesh—
so the ship did not reach harbour, lacking the élan
that blew fitfully in other passages. Eliot, blinded
by the necessity to defend the marriage-bond
as Anglicanly thought, forgot the *égoisme*
à deux of Antony and Cleopatra, ignored
"the still, sad music of humanity",

the various alones complaining to the alones,
lamenting the competitiveness of solos or duets
which became quintets unified by one theme
to drown that still, sad cry, faint as a reed
whispering to a tidal breeze in an obscure dyke
hidden by sea-front hotels and the sleek opulence
of closed Mercedes fouling the promenade.

Whose lust succeeded and whose failed does not matter.
The body absorbs and excretes but lives to express
a spirit: as Thomas Traherne would say,
that is what it is for. A memory's journey
is, like Isis searching through sea and desert,
a gathering of shards, a uniting of scattered love.

Dark girls behind doors, fair girls in shadowed alleys,
teachers and Socialist comets, I recollect
a famished boy partly in rags asking
in Heaton playground for the core of my apple:
I would have given him all and like Céline,
kindled by the dancing livingness of mischievous children
in the "kermesse de Wapping" or falling in love
with a girl of four "*en pleine grâce
et beauté blonde et santé*", though the boy
or since the boy was lithe in his torn trousers,
cheeky, sly, dirty, human with a wanton smile,
I would have selected him—but gave him my apple—
a sacramental apple, a Eucharist yearning—
that being more to the point, since he was hungry.

135

ENTR'ACTE

The active memory
must not
invent
but may
discover

                  (though finds become
                  statues when tenderly
                  disencrusted
                  as agate's identity
                  is polished):

vainly reproves
but can
constructively
lament;

must not impose
formalities
but may find
pattern.

A shingle bank
ridges, dips,
curves, hollows, points:
from jasper, slate,
waves build defence
against their own
destructiveness;

this we perceive,
record,
but did not
make it so.

136

(In pebbles hardness,
location, size
matter;

colour is extra.)

Broken rose quartz
edges dulled necessary flints
with rings of light.

The Triple Muses
daughters of Mnemosyne
made pebbles dance
to tell the future
without altering
the petrology.

ELEGY IV — ECLOGUE

In Memoriam Charles Péguy
Louis MacNeice and Pierre Emmanuel

A. You said you were not going to philosophise
or psychologise and spirit away
a real person—and yet you've quoted Céline
(dubious reading for one in charge of playgrounds)
and brought T. S. Eliot and Shelley in
with talk about Mnemosyne and the Triple Muse.

B. I know—but what concerns me is what the fact is,
what the real person is—though I remember
also what Plotinus said about lessening God.
Categories and schematisations must remain
forbidden if the myth behind what seems actual
is somehow to be perceived but not formalised
into something rigid. That's where Shelley went wrong,
like those he reproved for reproving: they were people.

Isabel Allende in *The House of the Spirits*
makes the President before his assassination
say that the heroine's grandfather, Esteban Trueba,
had his balls in the right place—and Alba loves him
and even understands (in the end) Esteban Garcia,
her illegitimate cousin, seeing what made him work
(even though the working made him torture and rape her):
after the climaxes she cannot find her hatred—
a chain of ritual is, as it has to be, broken.

A friend arrested in a political demonstration
was being sentenced and lectured by a magistrate
and almost became violent until he remembered
that this hectoring fool had recently lain in bed
beside his wife in possibly flimsy pyjamas
and probably had indigestion after Tory dinners.
He was born naked, had a bath naked, and might as well

be naked when he came to die. It is the suits,
the wigs, the accoutrements that take over people—
what Blake called "the states"—that are damnable:
the person is spirit, soul, being (call it what you will)
that got into this state and therefore suffers
even without knowing it, but who are we
to claim to know what he feels? The spirit is innocent.

A.   And you know that the difficulty of preserving
what you ironised as the décor is that Brother Ass
rebels and to get at the thistle pretends to be
an archetypal stallion or even a unicorn.

B.   We laugh at Monsieur Jourdain who didn't know
he'd been speaking prose all his life, but some
don't realise that they've been living poetry.
I doubt if it's worth while to pursue written poetry;
unless one is aware, as Chestov remarked,
that those who seek poetry are seeking more than poetry:
otherwise it's a marginal exercise like crossword puzzles.
Those who live poetry may rarely read it—
being occupied in the living—I am considering
how what is lived may be accurately expressed
in writing that's clear when read. There are two kinds
(for the purpose of this thought): the eternal,
Saint-Pol-Roux's ideorealism, the One that remains—
and the incidental outcry of those deprived,
the report on the world without hope, without knowledge,
man separated from the Earth and therefore from heaven.

We were real people in Shieldfield, the kids were real,
I was real enough, but we were unrooted,
débrouillard, lacking the rhythm of seasons, having red berries
in the time of blossoming. Edwin Muir described
the nightmare among city animals in a Glasgow bus,

James Thomson accurately expressed the dreadful night,
MacDiarmid diagnosed the urban disease and Alasdair Gray
unconsciously echoing Emmanuel's *Babel*
showed how the citizens of this alleged civilization
eat each other. Men have always eaten one another
(the basis of competition) but not as now
with efficient masking by certified additives.

Much begins with one of the most appalling
memoranda ever penned: Sir William Petty's "Wherefore—
leaving itt to God to punish the sin of women
who become with Child against his Commandments,
and leaving it to the world to punish such women
with Contempt and Dirision, leaving it
to the women themselves to suffer for their folly
in not obliging the men they deal with
to provide for their children—Lett the Government
in humanity make provision for every woman
with Child for 30 days, the woman leaving her child
to be a servant to the Government for 25 yeares
suppressing the names of their parents. The Charge
of maintaining a woman 30 days in Child bed
may well be defrayed for under 30 shillings,
but if the value of mankind be in this age & country
70£ per head, a new born Child, bread up to fair hard work
for 25 yeares, will be very well worth
3 times 30 shillings, as may be seen in the price
of Negroes children in the American plantations."

What is the value of mankind in this age and country?
More than in 1687? Or is the difference
accountable to the processes of inflation?

Were not two sparrows sold for a farthing?

Do not in this age of realpolitik alleged men
argued that you cannot make an omelette
without breaking eggs?

                    Were you in Shieldfield
cold in your daffodil frock out in the night air
after our sweaty dance, an egg to be broken,
a flower to be fried for guests in a Wordsworth hotel,
or a Child promising Social Profit as worth
3 times 30 shillings, bred up to hard work
for 25 yeares, except for unemployment,
firebombs or shrapnel in the alley? Or was your daughter
taken from you into Care, since the World punishes imprudence
with Contempt and derision, like Sir Wm Petty
leaving itt to God to punish the sin that was ours?

(Even through concrete and tarmac the Earth compels:
Notre Dame de Sous-Terre guard and succour your bed.)

A. Why do you speak to her who is probably dead
    instead of continuing dialogue? And what
    has the Black Madonna in Chartres to do with this?

B. Much, for what was born in me, as me,
    in the dingy streets among the sexy girls
    amid the hungry boys, was the receptive spirit,
    the needing spirit, awaiting her gospel, good news
    from the country of those whom history crucifies
    and the world derides or damns, since these are the children
    of the Mother of God, the genuine mother, begetting
    perpetually the seminal God, and Virgin
    being in the spirit innocent, as he is,
    and therefore the well of forgiveness in comprehension.

A Inasmuch as the seed that falls on the Earth grows
   and is what it is, can even her understanding
   turn tares to wheat so that the Shepherd's harvest
   neither wants nor needs that vengeful separation?

B. I do not know. If one knew one might
   become lulled by faith into inactivity.
   "All shall be well and all manner of thing shall be well"
   only if we remember that we are the hands
   and the wearied feet of what might make things well—
   though the feet of rescuing firemen may be burned
   and the hands caring for lepers become leprous.

   I remember selling programmes in the City Hall
   for the annual visit of the Glasgow Orpheus Choir
   (I could not afford a ticket) and—in spite
   of later strictures by the enraged MacDiarmid—
   I knew that there, through music which I had no knowledge
   to criticise or assess, came an inspiration:
   disturbingly puritan hymns were made beautiful, and
   from one devastated city to another
   there sounded the tune of hope, and Scottish islands
   (to me as unreal as Heaven) were sung to existence.
   I learned that "The Isle of Mull is of isles the fairest":
   I have walked on it since—but this is not a symbol
   but an indication of longing. I do not know
   whether Notre Dame de Chartres at all benefits
   the battered child in a Byker slum or if
   the beauty of Ardhasaig in the Isle of Harris
   exists in the world of that child, but the justification
   of art is, though tear-reddened eyes know nothing of either,
   the skirl of that child beseeching these things to be.

ELEGY V

Coming from Jesmond Dene on a twilit path
that edged a hillside field I saw above a bush
the face of a man, whose body was revealed
as frightened I passed by; his eyes threatened.
Looking back I realised that this was a trick
of light and imagination, like the two
people who once came down my street
as I waited by the gate at night. There have been others—
by open fencing and in smoke-filled rooms, resembling
those shadowy benevolent figures who came in the dark
to lean over my childhood bed. Was their comfort vain?
And how many people with whom I interchanged
glances or even words have not been there?
They may have comforted, too, unlike those in some rooms
who talked but in as true a sense as the wraiths
were not really there. It is dangerous to have
soliloquised conversations with imaginary beings
(girls, saints, or comforters) but equally dangerous
to converse with "real" persons who are not there,
though one mode may be insane, the other seem normal.
Thus we pass much of our brief life in dream
of one kind or another (the mad kind feeling better):
only when two generate a third, literally or "metaphorically"
(which here is a sort of literalness) or four make six
or seven, even more, has the Earth a voice
and the soul a life. Most of the time "society"
is characterised by being unsocial and a form
of refined cannibalism that is more horrific
than eating on tribal islands or in barbaric jungles.
(Cannibalism, a learned book once told me,
occurs only in savage societies that are
decayed civilisations, a religious rite—
dubious if fundamental—having become general
so that corruption somehow replaces the meaning.)

I awoke or was born in Jesmond or Shieldfield

143

into a world that only in snatches, encounters
in shaded alleys or behind ruins was other than bizarre.
I thank those who in classrooms or beside lampposts,
by the walls of goodsyards or in sweaty dances
achieved reality on the earth, on the tormented earth
that cries quietly for us to listen and to utter
what in our bone and flesh, our mind and spirit,
is its then articulate voice. The woods and waters
of the Ouseburn gorge and where its life becomes
partly obliterated or obscured in Byker and Shieldfield
asked, and the question or answer was repeated
time and again elsewhere, for people on the earth
to be the children of earth, not interlopers
from another system, who cannot talk or love
even among themselves. It would be vain to say
that all this was because of your limbs and your daffodil frock,
but I lament that you do not and cannot know
—since you are no longer that "you", I not that "I"—
what generated in one evening before the cold air
swirled frosty dust in gutters and between houses
of the fettered, imprisoned, thwarted family of earth,
the destined creators of heaven, yet builders of Babel.
It was not God who confounded their speech but the devil
that is in them because of the institutions of men,
the conventions of competition, the founded delusions
about what life is for: thus a gathering of people
on, say, Scalpay, or off the coast of Ireland
or by a lagoon in the Pacific may be meaningful life
which governments destroy to make history or financiers profit.

The living may not read this: written poetry
can, alas, in this Babel depend on the moribund
and may be replaced by fatal imitation,
articulated puppetry masquerading as action,
the creative Word obscured by invented words.

The Earth was conscious in us (we were two among many):
if it still is conscious in me, still conscious in you,
we are in one way together—but in another
the private bloods are perpetually separate
as bodies may lie in the same earth distinct
without power to know each other: identities,
like the purposes of Earth, its secret aim,
remain for our hindered minds mysterious,
not to be analysed this side of the tomb
and possibly not on the other, because the earth
may be the enigma that is all sides of the tomb,
joining what grieved to separately die.

The layered but severed dogwood is not one tree
yet cannot be wholly two. This elegy
is pure: it laments what cannot be remodelled, gilded
into fable or reincarnate, an ammonite in the shale
with nerves more tuned than at its origin.

I shall go in my mind (which is where all journeys are made)
to Sauveterre de Béarn, where ordinary streets
of humble houses neighbour the gracious and old
that edge the road to the *Place*. There a church and a wall
look over the gorge and see that the river
is half-crossed by a bridge that's remained unfinished
for centuries. Lizards on the warm stone
bask or dart in the sunlight, not knowing the legends.

We were like lizards but darted in the damp air—
which nonetheless was the heat in the old adage,
"Thou out of heaven's benediction com'st
To the warm sun"—and at Sauveterre
from heat I can seek the blessing from which I come.
This alien land is where I have found home—
As also at Chapel Stile, where the slate houses

145

climb the slate hill beside derelict Thrang Quarry
and people have their own life and visitors wander
briefly among them to replenish the soul
since both love the independent and friendly crags
which would kill them if there's no respect in their love,—

or Sandwick near Ullswater and Martindale
in the place where there is no road through but a way
there (for the sane)—

            or Lindisfarne which connects
with the busy world but is twice a day cut off
to be what it is—

        for these are places
where with my fellow-pilgrim and our children
(and thus a "we" not an "I") a complex mind
has alternated between the shade of the altar
and the frenzied inspiriting wind, the fervid sun,
the pitiless snow, the hail, and that evening peace
which heals, for example, loud storms on the Isle of Mull.

AN IMAGE HAS NO HANDS;
VARIATION ON THE BEGINNING OF THE
FIRST CONVERSATIONAL ELEGY

In a story that's torn out from the second paragraph
one remembers that starring sentence in the first,
narrating a dance expressive of discovered harmony,
and ignores that the fifth, sixth, seventh
would be cacophonous and page twelve probably lead
to a stark end like the novel we've just closed.

I remember the feel of the coarse brown cloth on your back
and you underneath responding in spite of it;
and below all was your dark triangle, a masked image
like a statue unclear in a dim chapel—but it was others,
puritan or salacious, who dreamed motives—
that wasn't what we'd just found and were about to lose.

Paths that join by chance by hazard diverge
and fiction and fact being what are now too familiar,
we should have become what we are now, concerned
with people who don't respond as we hope, and want
what we didn't expect or provide for; for you in this,
as those I love now, I can do nothing.

You became, of course, an eternal: it essentialises
in other persons, other acts, but no one
feels inside a symbol or finds comfort as a theme.
The point about eternity is that it isn't now,
as it wasn't then. Eternity has no arms
to hold one till one finds words, and it is speechless.

We are all in a maze barriered by distances
of space and time, by emotions and remembered emotions.
Could we not amalgamate into one pilgrimage
to a Sunday School happy land, and not merge
as scrunched bones in the maw of the minotaur?

Human persons can become standing stones on a moor,
ground-fixed so they cannot support one another: warm flesh
on their sentient skeletons is replaced by lichen of weathering,
moss rooted in lines grooved by blown rains of erosion.
To some, perhaps to themselves, they seem distorted shapes,
their limbs ungainly, their brows fierce, their faces baleful.
None knows that garnets within them jewel magetic ore
since lines of force lose themselves in peat and pebbles
among the glare of sharp spar and fractured edges of flints.

That was not the hearts' rhythm in the admired sentence;
it is not the heart's rhythm now, which no feet dance.

People decribed in a paragraph did not write it.

VI

LATER POEMS

CHILD OF MNEMOSYNE

"Put that tray on the floor," he said. "Now take your robe off, and come into this bed, which is your bed and Dan's, whose place I've only borrowed for a moment, whether in bed, or in your hidden places, or in your life."
(*He* is Matthew in *Voices of Children* by Edward Candy, Gollancz, 1980, p. 148.)

Muse, I know you are not mine: I borrow
your secret places and tomorrow
you'll belong to others while I follow
your footsteps into empty houses.

I am as briefly yours but we are faithful
like waiting Magdalene during the fateful
colloquies till Easter. We are grateful
(both, I hope) that the sluices

watering various gardens can be cleared
of the dead leaves and mucus that mired
what should always be limpid. We heard
in sundry incarnations the voices

that echoed one voice. Lovers embody
(fleetingly) love so they become ready
when it grows whole. Unsteady
as a toddler each of us chooses

to fall in learning to walk. We change
with dawn, noon and sunset; we range
like domestic ducks on the scrounge
for adventure in new watery spaces.

But since we both left the home yard
wandering through wanton byways which lured
to strange and carnal knowledge, we shared
and share the twilight aurora that fuses

tree, tomb, stream, cloud in a cadence that as it closes
modulates to the ninth mode, the lasting word.

151

BRIDGE OVER THE OUSEBURN, JESMOND DENE

The swallows have flown through the bright sunshine
away from the midnight frosts, since earth and the planets turn
cyclic like Ouseburn water lovely over stone
accidentally as it falls through slums to the Tyne
and flows to the sea to evaporate into rain
and glint incidentally on haphazard rocks again.
The swallows will come back. The girls and I are gone.

No one remembers Freda, Brenda, Betty
as their limbs and spirit felt. In records of the city
deeds or deaths may be dustily filed. But in maps
that accurately trace rivers no water flashes,
lakes do not ripple, there are no shadows. Cups
once emptied never hold the same wine again: blushes
recur but are never that first complicity
with you, fecund earth, in fortuitous generosity.

We were briefly your voices, were briefly the ear
that listened, not always attentively, to what
you were always saying and will every cyclic year
whisper, shout, laugh or lament when we are not.
Let others who, feeling, speak know you also hear.

SLUM DOCUMENTARY — SHOT 45

In that photograph I recognise a face,
your mother and the son we never had—
he not much younger than the you I knew.
I'm happy both seem well, though times were bad
when this was taken. Someone somehow won through,
anyway, to something resembling grace,

though expressed in china ornaments and chairs
with unfrayed arms, different from those you hated
but thought were normal when you ran around
barefoot, with tousled hair, joy unabated
in eyes that flashed like a blue oasis found
sunlit in stormy sky—Why, none knew. None now cares.

Memories of backstreets etch barred shadow clear;
what happened behind is vague—a clue is lost,
a person vanishes and is replaced
by fantasy. This realist print has glossed,
with furniture and subjects neatly spaced,
the rough-hewn sadness that you are not there.

I — FAREWELL TO BRENDA HJERSING

You ' could not come' but someone else
was behind St. Mary's Chapel.
Let connoisseurs flatter a ripening peach
by deriding a rough-skinned apple.

She had not flowing yellow hair,
Norwegian sea-blue eyes,
fingers that touched like gossamer,
or a voice that hallowed lies.

But in autumn twilight any gaze
that's warm and somehow freed
from moral fetters is welcoming
to a boyish body's need.

Her lips were full—if unrefined
compared with yours; they gave.
I could not feed on height of mind
with no one there to save

from dark streets curving on and on
or straight streets hard with light,
rich people happily affable
and the poor hunched cold or to let.

It was not love, but what she did
her willing boyfriend knew—
as I, since she was who she was
and someone else was you.

II — LETTER FROM BRENDA HJERSING

I said I'd come but could not come:
my mother would not let me out.
My voice was gentle with the truth—
to try to ease that awful doubt

which drove your footsteps down each street
where haunted eyes made shadows twirl,
so that you dangerously sought
rebirth from every frightened girl.

It was the heat within your gaze
that cooled my blue eyes like the sea,
so you could bathe your care, and laze
in what was, innocently, me.

But since we never met again—
rather than grieve to untwist your stare
I wrapped less complicated men
in wavelets of my yellow hair.

THRENODY FOR A ROSE

Spare a thought, you who pass these
autumnally battered floribundas,
pruned of their hope of berries,
for Rose La Touche, the precocious
child-pet of Ruskin, whom she addressed
gaily, affectionately as St. Crumpet,
and from whom she learned much about art
in relation to life but possibly too little
about life and what art would set it free.

With a mind darkened by Puritan theology—
her father loving too much in concepts from Spurgeon
and her mother too jealous to comprehend
anorexia or the child as well behaved minx—
she became Proserpine with parental Pluto
and her lover a male Demeter half demented.

She died and there were no more rose-petals
instead of letters, and inane messages
in séances did not relight her eyes
nor recreate the sensation of her skin.

Lament, again, not only Victorianly
but also in this and in every year
that Spring's rich flowering into episodic Summer
is overcome annually by the starving snow.

Roses may bloom again but not that rose.

LINDISFARNE

"When we compare the present life of man with that time of which we have no knowledge,
it seems like the swift flight of a lone sparrow through the banqueting hall in the winter
months ... while he is inside, he is safe from the winter storms; but after a few moments
of comfort he vanishes from sight into the darkness whence he came." Bede, II, 13

Nothing will come of loving this island:
like all things holy it is not in the world
of market-place technology you're compelled
to live in. Cold, bleak, tide-fettered, it survives
as a quaint home for fishermen and a brief halt
for coaches of trippers doing Northumbrian castles
and snapping odd slides to enliven talks at soirées.

It was in fact always thus: after all, Aidan
is now a statue difficult to photograph without
a pub as background. Northumbria was evangelised
but now Newcastle hardly exhibits salvation.
The Lindisfarne Gospels (that were saved from the sea)
interest few except as an artistic curiosity
hardly relevant, say, to African famine,
and the saintly disciples journeyed with Cuthbert's bones
over snow-swirled fells and fire-swept years to Durham
without fixing in minds as fickle as flame or frost
what would now save the streets new pirates ravage
or feed their kitten-limbed girls and disappointed men.

But I have been thinking of Aidan and Cuthbert
in this modern context: they would inquire
what will come of the technology, the market economy
and the people they thwart, dominate, twist— the girls
and the men who should delight their characteristic nubility.
The life of man is still what it was. An image
brought boats of crystal-minded men, till the transit
of relics fleeing Viking raiders who themselves

157

soon sought the illumination those gospels offered.
Technology tells us no more than the sparrow in the hall.

So I will go on the dunes, seek marram and lyme-grass,
the loneliness of blown sand, curlew, peewit and fulmar,
the wisps of saintliness—and praise this island.
A marsh pool between gale-hollow hills is as central
as the Stock Exchange and something will come of
worshipping this air's clarity with profitless love.

INCANTATION AT ILKLEY

Before the organisational man, Lady,
before the analyses of time and syntheses of law
for the computers of morality and the calculators of profit,
you, triple because not solely one
not simple, single-minded, but
hooded so that you cannot be categorised,
castellated with outcrop to gather a view of the world,
the spires rising from earth to pierce mist to beyond earth—

You of the ring involving also the serpent,
Chalice healing the broken spear and welding the
                                        cracked ploughshare—

Mother who gives birth and dancing girl
who enlightens with the nymph's promise
and she who at the end washes the body of stain,
hallowing the coming, the journey, the going—

Hollow in the rock, marks that give earth a face
humanising the stone—

Patroness of the well and the river snaking through the dale,
herdsmaid of the milch cattle feeding the child,
old woman with the oxcart homing with the evening sun—

Now, when dawn lights raindrops on the iris
that echoes your patterns on the curve of the leaf:
Now, when noon dries the dew on the boulder
where men carved your symbol on what was hard:
Now, at midnight when moths finger warm curls in what is cold:
Now, meaning at every time since you are timeless,
fold us in your forgiveness, you who are Isis
reintegrating the body of him who is scattered;
grant us your integrity, virgin yet mother;
illuminate our disbelief, harlot become saint;
protect us and our children, madonna whom the oppressed
dug stained from darkening compost and clinging clay—

So that we may thwart the desecrators, the poisoners,
destructors who diabolise the nuclei of living—
from soil, from peat, from gravel, from obdurate strata
construct the conviction that this place where we dwell
is the timbered temple with the hazel twig, the hawthorn blossom,
the hearth for the fire of our being.

ARAINN —
THE ARRAN POEM

Oyster-catcher of Catacol
busy among the etched and fluted rocks
you do not know what poison radiates
from these pellucid waters

Cuckoo skimming Meal nan Damh*
speckled flickering focus of dappled bracken
you call without perceiving
what your romantic minor havocs echo

Blackback winnowing over calm Kilbrannan*
Gannet poised on Imachar's* gnarled stack
you do not recognise the metal birds
that shoot past with smooth omen

Buzzard of Beinn Bharrain*
circling with narrowing serenity
you will not pity what your gifted eyes
see for your glide to kill

Grey seal of Lochranza* sleek on the lucent schist
you do not heed the subtle engines
that churn beneath the waves that dip to rise
and counterchange the shimmering sea

---

*   *Notes on Pronunciation and Meaning:*
Meal nan damh (male nan dav), hill of the stag, near Glen Catacol;
Killbrannan (An Caolas Brandanach), strait of St. Brendan, between Kintyre and Arran;
Imachar (eemachar, stress first syllable) originally 'Iomaire', ridge of land;
Beinn Bharrain (Ben Varen) mountain with gap between two peaks;
Lochranza is said to mean 'loch of the rowan trees'.

Eider of Sannox[*] paddling tranquil water
past the massive landslips of conglomerate
you mate outside the mystery
of cataclysmic aeons

Red Deer from Suidhe Fhearghas[*]
you browse beyond deserted mines
ignoring where light finer grasses edge
lost homes of evicted men whose music vanished

Curlew near the high brown stones of Machrie[*]
bubbling of Spring round a solemn autumnal place
you need not know how on a foreign hill
Christ died and why the watching women wept

---

*

Sannox comes from Old Norse for 'sandy bay';
Suidhe Fhearghas (sooye eryes) shelf where Fergus rested;
Machrie means machair.

INDWELLER

He was eighty, so I was told, and lived alone
in the only habitable house in the south of Ardnish
as total population of Glasnacardoch
and Peanmeanach, where there had been a school
for the children of crofters, while elderly cottagers
would come down to meet the boat from Lochailort
and join merry music of language. There was no road
to those places, just as no road from the loch head
went by Irine and Roshven to Glenuig
and round to Kinlochmoidart, as it now does:
its new communication abolished the old—
once no roads but a boat, now only a road
one side of the seaway, so that what had united
became a barrier, the serviceable water
severing, as though the words of friendliness
suddenly changed meaning and alienated.
One came to hear mainly English south of those waves
over which every morning the innkeeper
would focus his binoculars to see if the old man
was about in his garden or emptying the ash—
and in the evening would look for the living light.
I suppose that one day he missed the signs
and got out his boat not to ferry supplies.

I do not know if when others left he stayed
or had gone there seeking a home for recollections
but he either was or made a memorial—
and more than that: he established an entity,
an embodied soul in a world, what each of us
in fact is, along with the seagull, the wagtail, the mouse,
an aliveness among the stones and possibly
in the mystery of this earth something more
than the butterfly, an alertness that can speak
even though no one apparently hears. To him
whatever replied (if it did) might be as valuable
as the conversations in Trafalgar Square

162

or Westminster debates to cut subsidies
to communications no longer viable
for peninsulas whose sole dividend is love.

BLAEN DIGEDI
(Bendigedig[*])

Innumerable streams. Two small fords. The downhill
road turns just past them and rises
away among trees. Looking back, the traveller
glimpses through branches Y Twmpa seemingly vertical,
bleak, grassed but browned with sheer rock, shadowed
with purple above lush green near many waters.

---

*   *Bendigedig* means blessed.

A sudden exultation lightens the burden
within the being, as though the earth had spoken
what religious rituals call comfortable words.
But there had been merely a turning of the head,
a glance to the road taken, a pause in a journey
a photograph where others had frequently been—
a notice saying "Please take your litter home", implying
that some forgot sacredness as disconcerting.

                                              Yet
after long silence not broken by the admiration
of mountains glistening with ice, snowslopes, and trees
both shapely and gnarled, twisted into curious angles
that seemed meaningful, there came, without prelude
or apparent justification, this utterance, as though
some friend believed to be voyaging far off
opened a door to say "I'm back", sat down
and poked to inspirit dying embers.

                                    To respond
by inventing theology would fossilise a god
as soul-fettering idol, but to pass on
as though nothing had occured would wreak pseudo-science
like a vandal splashing and daubing a pensioner's garden,
newly planted and seeded, with stolen creosote.

Merely yet mainly I shall now remember
this place: innumerable streams; two fords; the road
among trees below the rockface, and I shall know,
even dying, not something stated, but a presence
that was also a promise, of which it is not granted
to phrase, vaguely or particularised, a definition.

THE MAKE-UP BOX

(A riverbank in El Salvador echoing the China Sea)

The fleeing have faces. The commentary
measuring words on political reality
cannot prevent the momentary
impact of their humanity.

Once, their eyes watched limbs crowding
their boat on the unforgiving
unhating sea, while hoarding
the fluid hopes of their living
in clefts of brain and body they drifted
like green twigs in a torrent—a stone
or a surge could be final. Wafted
by once welcome wind they sank to bone
alongside reefs (dead sticks).
                                                        And now others
whose nakedness earns no wages turn
taut eyes to the camera among the protective
leaves by the sundering river. Homes burn
behind them. The dawn sun was detective
of their obstinate persistence in having brothers,
parents, friends, a lover. The collective
terms of the commentary clothe their faces
in eye-shadow and foundation cream of 'forces'.

A happier picture follows—the well-dressed
whose prepared masks talk and smile, cosmetic
in cheek, mouth, limb and phrase, to greet a guest
simulated like pilot-training in static
battle schools. Faces, limbs, eyes
need civil cover. She lies,
that child, cold now, near the stark
defoliated trees the wrong side
of the river. The dark
water laps her while the financial news
tells those in soft-lit rooms it's time for bed.

FOR EPHRAIM MTHETWA

"A Black South African standing trial on security charges died in a Durban gaol yesterday. The prison service said that Ephraim Mthetwa, aged 22, from the Lamontville black township had apparently committed suicide by hanging himself with his tracksuit jacket."
— Reuter. *The Guardian*, 'News in Brief', 27th August 1984.

I do not know you, what you did or what
the security forces said you'd done: you are
an item in *News In Brief.* I gather
that the Danes export pornography, that Borg's girlfriend
is or is not pregnant, that Noah's Ark
has been found on Mount Ararat, and a Bulgarian
has swum one thousand three hundred miles down the Danube.
Prince Franz Josef II of Liechtenstein
has given his power to his son, and a Cypriot tanker
previously on fire has been towed to a Persian island.
Eight people have recently been killed on roads near Malaga.
Four Bangladeshi fishermen have been shot by Indian
security forces, and Authorities will soon
begin more talks about Namibian independence.
A South African aged one-twenty recommends
no wine or tobacco but lots of red meat.
I set these things down as it is necessary
to see your death in some kind of context
as I resume pointing my house wall. You are
one of thirteen corpses fallen like dollops
of surplus cement. Any garden seems Ararat—
present, not archaeological: a dove
would find an olive twig in each one
and be mistaken. The flood has not subsided
but became what it should destroy, like security forces.
We are all very far from the Caucasus, with no ark.

FORTH-CLYDE EXPRESS

A ruined angular tower on a rocky hillock
glimpsed from a train among small, steep valleys
and little brown moors, though the general landscape
was pastorally green: I could not name it—
I searched maps but had forgotten placarded stations
before and after. I have seen it three times since—
always with surprise and an odd longing
to be in its story, though it is possible
that I would not wish to belong there if suddenly
the urgent dream came true. Why should I rejoice
to know now it is Niddry Castle except to create
an identity in what newspapers call history?

The rails we run on take us past the places
we would inhabit. I remember an Estonian girl
whom I never met since I missed that job in Tallin.
We prefer the imaginary to the real
because we can alter it; but even then
some kind of track takes over—Russian invasion,
blizzards or feuding lairds. On the whole
the imagination's function is to be in the carriage
concerned for the child too small to work the magic
of the automatic doors, her sobs clawing for handles.

What kind of doors did this rust-red tower have?
Who glimpsed what through those window-holes before
this railway was built and called the permanent way?

ORKNEY BUS

Mr Ward of Derby looking through the window
of the Stromness-Kirkwall bus at his tenth glimpse
of the Stones of Stenness, the Ring of Brogar
and the light over heath and water, told me
about them and his longer explorations
which made this annual brief sight ecstatic.

The first Summer he had come with his dear wife,
the second alone. He would come every year
though now he merely walked about in Kirkwall—
even that was enough to fill all fifty
weeks spent in his little garden in Derby,
those few square yards behind a terraced cottage.

God, when, looking at great men and states, you think
to burn the world, pray to Mr Ward of Derby.

AFTER TV NEWS

For these masters
dawn, noon, night drooped
impoverished,
clear springs muddied,
boys killed, girls whored,
old men cramped cried
last bitter hours.

Righteous, they smile
unctuously
on hotel stairs.

LE CHEMIN DES ECOLIERS

Photograph by Willy Ronis (1954)

Three hooded figures move away like little black Graces
to a school that is near the horizon that mists obscure.
If they turned to us and had gnarled benevolent faces
we would bow to the Mothers carved in miniature.

That is of course what we should do, even though
they are girls in a lonely lane. The oncoming car,
the telephone poles, the fences, and what they grow
in classrooms to believe as the things that are

might be part of the cold their cloaks and stockings keep out:
inside is the warm smell of their bodies, and one
seems to be whispering. Though diffused, the light
makes their shadows on the staring road a dark sun.

WHITE WAGTAIL ON A LAWN, CONISHOLME OLD RECTORY

> *"God made everything out of nothing, but the nothingness shows through."* Paul Valéry —
> Mauvaises pensées et autres *(1942)*

Canon Longley could scythe a croquet lawn
more neatly than modern machines,
his beard waving in a sea-wind over the marsh
as the blade swung
a tune above the ground-swish of the reeds.

He is nothing now
except an item of social history,
an image with no substance
or meaning.

"Vanity of vanities ..."
he would have remembered.

Early this century
he came from Pontefract,
but decades before that
from nowhere.

But it was something
to smooth from a quagmire
as squelchy as primordial chaos
that formality
to scythe,

to paint in water-colour
on waste paper
without a mad child's scribbles
or the housekeeper's shopping list
showing through,

or to identitfy
motacilla alba alba
and briefly share
the jaunty balance of that unquestioning
temerity.

STROLLING IN THE GARDEN

(After emptying a damp cupboard)

Skylark—seeming to climb
an invisible spiral stair
where quivering wings create
landings in air,
impelled to struggle and sing
by energies innate
or learned that I won't presume
to fathom or annotate—

I—who today have read
papers hidden in a file
decade by decade—can dare
to claim one parallel
in the otherwise different:
climbing a mythical stair
men wing words to pretend
landings in air.

EPIPHANIES

Picking up the Yorkshire Post while waiting
for the next client—a marital problem
more complex than his own—he read
. that sand martins had reached some other place
where, unlike where he was, there were cliffs
with curving hollows sheltered by overhang:
soon there would be swallows swerving over the yard—
he loved their colour, grace and skilful motion.

A fortnight later, dictating, he asked his secretary
what he could say to a friend who needed
not only advice but news of how things went,
as though between gossip and bits of family chat
a correspondent might slip a divine message:
"Any important events?" "No, nothing's happened
except that I saw swallows three days ago
using the telephone wires to celebrate arrival.
After their difficult journey it was a pity
that it snowed in the afternoon and froze that night."
"Tell me immediately when you see a swift," he pleaded
remembering how, once, walking from office to car-park,
he had looked up to see, with high purpose over darkening buildings,
a tern that knew of some far estuary.

ON THE WAY TO THE BEACH
(EASTINGS, NEAR FRAMGORD, UNST)

We decided it was the skull
of a seal, not a sheep. Someone
had set it on the top of a grassy hump
like a miniature memorial on an eminence
beside the path to the colourful beach
—grass, serpentine-tinted sand, grey stone
and a sea variegated green and blue.
Somehow there was in the shape
that sentimental benevolence that seals
seem to people to have and we put it back
reverently on its little knoll. The image
of it is in my mind now and an emotion
I cannot describe as a thought but wish I could.
That something was and is not is hardly
worth stating again, but why do I remember
what since I never knew it I could not and cannot forget?

LODGING WITH TIME IN THE NENT VALLEY

Old but sparrow-sprightly, she promised to knock
at seven-thirty every morning so I could wade
through deep snow to school breakfast, never late—
though she had no watch and the cottage no clock.

In a storm by night, when hail rattled the panes
of my window her sleep-walking husband waved a candle
wildly over my bed, till she guided him back
saying it was twenty past two (my watch still gains

as it did then). Once when the bus was late
and she had done the Winter's shopping a week early
since drifts would soon block the road, she failed to stop him
barrowing crow-coal from the tunnel-mound by the far gate.

She walked for oil after that, but he had caught
the chill that made him bedfast. Though a nephew came
to help with the stairs, one morning she wryly said,
"It's five to twelve—I can rest," sat down, and died.

THE HUMAN VARIATIONS

I
PROLOGUE: EADFRITH'S SAINT MATTHEW
(LINDISFARNE GOSPELS)

The life infusing eye and hand
that limned this saint red, gold and green
was meticulous craft in faith and not
the normal urge of blood and bone.

Tools served an incandescent mind:
though a candle dies with wick and wax
and the brush falls when the heart stops
colours outlast the body's tricks

sanctified in a world that burns
but lights no faith. A car wheel turns
guided in power but its final course
havocs when changed to mindless force;

yet this illumination glows
in beauty and for believers hope,
as when a slattern bears a Christ
annunciated during rape.

II
THE ALLENDALE SWAN
(Metal Swan crafted in Allendale)

This swan will last longer than what it models
in cold metal tooled to imitate the form
of feathered flesh and bone, wings set in flight,
the head tilted to navigate, while the tail
slightly inclines to a turn. A craftsman
made it to seem living, but had
to contrive apparent buoyancy by fixing
its right wing-tip in a piece of slate,
so summarising Allendale and the people there:
in and on what lasts longer than they
houses are built and lives enact
the fiction of their being—always
subtly grounded to permit a pretence to fly.

III
STRAIT-LACING
(Antony and Cleopatra I.iii.71)

"Cut my lace, Charmian." Cleopatra,
who was in fact pretending to pretend,
had no corsets and Shakespeare
no historical sense—in politics
or fashion—but he knew
the body beneath the clothing, the feeling
(heart, soul, nerve-endings) within the body.
My images are cliché or physiology;
his show how truly for any period
he had a sense of history, the way
human persons suffer within events.

IV
SMALL LOG ON THE KENT ESTUARY

It looks like a frog changing into a tortoise
but is itself—wood that grew to a form
which would smooth or hollow in the river's flow
and have its knobs etched by the tide
moving over sand and stones. It becomes,
like harebells that are difficult for gardeners
to grow but can seed themselves on shelly dunes,
or mica that can flash black or silver
and satifyingly be. But for that significance
all need a watcher who will find more
than what caused their evolution, formation or texture;
otherwise they unknown and unknowingly exist
in an elsewhere that for no one is somewhere.
What happens when the observer's thought, proved mortal,
isn't anywhere?

V
EPILOGUE: THE HARROWING OF HELL
(Saxon carving in Bristol Cathedral)

Halo'd, robed, Christ attracts upward
the petitioning naked person,
the nakedness not revealing the sex, for this
is vulnerable, aspirant animal, innocent
though by the artist's theme in Hell:
the spirit yearning in flesh, through flesh, knows
that it is also flesh, and redemption
is the flesh finding the spirit and the soul
reconciling the body without which
it seems not to be.

Clothe us, Lord, though so that we know
what, naked, is underneath, and what
beauty, dream, deed
justifies
                        or destroys.